God's Power In The Believer

O'Neal Stallworth Porter

God's Power In The Believer

O'Neal Stallworth Porter

Oh Kneel Publishing

Unless otherwise indicated all Scripture quotations are taken from the King James Version of the Holy Bible. Please note that **Oh Kneel Publishing Company's** publishing style capitalizes pronouns in Scripture that refer to the Father, Son, and Holy Spirit, and may differ from some Bible publishers' styles.

God's Power in The Believer
ISBN: 978-0-9777329-1-3
Copyright 2011 by Oh Kneel Publishing

P.O. Box 13125
Eight Mile, Alabama 36633
(251) 281-7643
Email: ohkneelpublishing@yahoo.com

Printed in the United States of America. All rights reserved under International Copyright Law. Contents and/or cover may not be reproduced in whole or part in any form without the expressed written consent of the Publisher.

CONTENTS

Acknowledgments	7
Dedication	9
Foreword – Dr. Leonard Scott	11
Introduction	13
1 - Power?	17
2 - Whose Power?	35
3 - But Ye Shall Receive Power	45
4 – From Whence Cometh This Power	57
5 - Where's The Power?	67
6 - Power In Practice	79
7 - More Power	91
8 - Spirit-Filled, Not Spirit-Led?	101
9 - Dunamis In Your Life	107
The Work Of The Holy Ghost	115
10 – The Baptism Of Power	117
Spirit Filled Confession	131
Personal Note	133
Biography	135
Contact Info	136

Acknowledgements

Thanks be unto God for His awesome revelation and faithfulness in entrusting me with His Word.

To my wife, Sabrina, and my children, Kymberly, Brooke, Morgan and Charles, (granddaughter, Amber and nephew, Isaiah) thank you for sharing me with the world. Your continual support and faithfulness to kingdom work has encouraged and strengthened me to effectively continue to proclaim the gospel in multi-faceted ways.

Thank you for friends coming through to assist me in the success of this publication: Yvonne Reed Matthews and Michael Green, editing; Charles Andrews (Indygo Media), cover design; Darius O'Cain, technical assistance; Alton Stephens, Minister Sharyl Jackson and Pastor Terrance Bulger, ongoing spiritual and emotional re-enforcement.

To the saints of God at Fellowship Church affectionately called "THE SHIP", thank you for allowing me to serve you for the past 21 years. I am humbled and blessed to minister unto you as your pastor. God has done great things over the past two decades. I believe the best is yet to be made manifest. Continue being true to your slogan: "A Perfecting Place, For Imperfect People".

Dedication

This volume is dedicated to my spiritual sons and daughters in ministry who are doing great exploits in the kingdom of God and making strides of excellence in the earth realm. I challenge you to continue to embrace the investment of God's Word in your lives and your ministry. Always be led by the Spirit in all that you say and do. The Baptism in The Holy Ghost is real and is as relevant today as it was in the early church. Continue to minister this precious gift of God to those whom God blesses you to reach.

It blesses me and encourages me when you make reference to me as your spiritual Father. It is an humbling position to be blessed to pour into the lives of others. I pray that your life and ministry have been even better blessed as God has used me to mentor you in your spiritual assignment. And most of all, I pray that our Heavenly Father is glorified in all that we do in the Name of His Son Jesus Christ through the power of the Holy Ghost in the earth realm.

Pastor Christopher Wilson
Senior Pastor, Church Of The Harvest

Minister Dorothy Thompson
Associate Minister, Fellowship Church

Evangelist Georgia Lawson
Associate Minister, Fellowship Church

Pastor Ivan Williams
Senior Pastor, Park City Chapel

Minister Sharyl Jackson
Associate Minister, Fellowship Church

Foreword
By Bishop Leonard Scott

Power is defined as the possession of a controlling influence, or the possession of the qualities required in doing something or getting something done. Synonyms for power include control, effectiveness, jurisdiction, persuasiveness, potency, strength, energy, might, force, ability, authority, competency, productivity, dominance, capability, and vigor.

Power is crucial to communication competency, the resolution of conflicts and the achievement of individual goals. A power resource is a resource that helps with the achievement of goals. This book is such a resource.

Power is that which makes action possible. Power can be held through delegation, social class, wealth, personal or group charisma, expertise, ability or skills, persuasion, knowledge, celebrity, force, violence, coercion, religion, group dynamics such as public relations, or social influence of tradition. These describe the power that can be wielded by man, which at best is limited. But what happens when man taps into God's power which is unlimited, God being omnipotent? In the following pages you will receive insights from the very knowledgeable Pastor O'Neal Porter concerning this awesome opportunity in the Lord.

Bishop Leonard Scott is the founder and president of the nation's oldest black owned gospel recording company, Tyscot, Inc. He is also the pastor of Rock Community Church in Indianapolis, Indiana.

Introduction

Many believers are unnecessarily hindered and defeated in their Christian walk simply because of a misconception of one word – **power**. I have seen too many well-intentioned believers who feel as if the power that they so desperately need in order to bring about change in their lives is somewhere in the heavenlies. If God made a promise that *"ye would receive power,"* then it is time for that power to be realized and made manifest.

This is a wake-up call to stir believers to recognize the indwelling presence of God "ready, willing, and able" to equip and empower you to excel. Yes, God has already empowered you – it's now time for you to realize and recognize what God has already done and walk in victory in every area of your life. No longer search for something on the outside that God has already deposited on the inside.

Do not allow the fact that you still have flesh issues hinder the progressive work that God is doing. I understand that there may be many things undone. Areas in your life may need attention. But, until the "outside search" for answers is called off and the inner search for truth is activated, true deliverance will not take place. The devil does his best to cause life's problems to divert attention from the true treasure that lies within every believer.

Religion has encouraged us to sing until the power comes down and pray until the power comes down. Nothing is wrong with singing or praying – they are both biblically correct activities that every Christian should take a part. However, when these are the only methods used to see the manifestation of the power of God something is desperately wrong.

There is a simple process of bringing into manifestation the promises of God: Read, Believe, Say, and Do! Read God's Word. God's Word is infallible. It cannot lie. It does not change. Whatever God has decreed in His Word must come to pass. Then you must believe what you read. No matter what you experience in life, it should not deter your faith in God's Word. Then begin to recite God's Word. Release it into the atmosphere. Make positive affirmations about yourself to change your attitude and environment. Read it out loud so that you can hear it. **"Faith comes by hearing, and hearing by the Word of God."** You must embrace God's Word that you read and hear. And believe that not only is it true, but that it is true for you. And the critical action is to "do" God's Word. If you have read it, believed it, and said it: it is very important that you follow up by doing the Word of God.

No longer should you be reaching and stretching upward to get something to come down. If you are a born again believer then the Spirit of God resides within you. According to the Book of Romans, Chapter 8 and verse 9, *"Ye are not in the flesh, but in the Spirit, if so be that the Spirit of God dwell in you. Now if any man have not the Spirit (life, breath) of Christ, he is none of His."* And as God promised in the Book of Acts that you would receive power after that the Holy Ghost had come UP – on you!

It's Time To Learn How To Reach Inward!

That's right, begin speaking the Word of Faith and activate the Spirit of God which resides within you. Within you there is a river. Allow the rivers of living water to flow out of your belly. The rivers are symbolic of the Spirit of God. Allow the Spirit to come UP from your innermost being (your spirit man) and begin to anoint every part of you!

This is God's perfect will for every believer! God wants HIS POWER to be made manifest in you. Although, you may feel as if you aren't really deserving or worthy – you're not! But thank God for His grace, His mercy, His agape love, His compassion, His lovingkindness, tendermercies, patience, longsuffering, forbearance... and the list continues. God even said in His word that *"we are all as an unclean thing, and our righteousnesses are as filthy rags; and we all do fade as a leaf, and our iniquities, like the wind, have taken us away".* (Isaiah 64:6)

Yet, God still wants His power made manifest in you. The scriptures even declare that *"we have this treasure in earthen vessels, that the excellency of the power may be of God and not of us".* (II Corinthians 4:7)

As you read this book, expect a new insight into Biblical principles and scriptural discoveries. Invite the Holy Spirit to renew your mind to receive revelation knowledge. Begin to put into practice the fundamentals of the Word of God and see a different manifestation of the anointing and release of God's Power in your life.

Power?

It's raining cats and dogs and you are stranded in the middle of the night on a deserted stretch of highway. You are sitting in the driver's seat of your newly purchased vehicle. Yet, each time you turn the key, nothing happens! You need power!

You own a piece of property on the other side of town. Someone (without your permission) has erected a makeshift building and is living on your property. You ask them to move it, but they ignore you! You need power!

According to Webster's Dictionary, power is defined as possession of control, authority, or influence over others; ability to act or do; legal or official authority, capacity, or right; physical might; force or energy that is or can be applied to work. All of these are correct definitions; but for a clearer spiritual understanding, let's take a look at the Word of God and discuss two common Greek terms for the word power.

Two Greek words used when referring to the word power are *exousia* and *dunamis*. *Exousia* means privilege, authority or jurisdiction. In Matthew 28:18, Jesus told His disciples that, **"All power is given unto me in heaven and in earth."** In the Amplified Bible, this verse is rendered, **"All authority (all power of rule) in heaven and on earth has been given to me."** Jesus is saying that He now has the legal right to bring about control not only in the heavenlies, but in the earth realm as well. When He paid the ultimate sacrifice on Calvary and rose from the grave with power and victory, the earth realm rights were stripped from the devil. Jesus, your elder brother, is the legal one in charge. God has also given this power to you as well. Remember, you are joint heirs with Christ. And God has blessed you with this same authority.

It may surprise you that Jesus had to "pay a price" for *exousia*. Most just assume that because of whom He is (the Son of God), that he already had it. But, what you must understand is that God is a God of order. In Genesis, *exousia* (rule, authority, dominion) had been given to man through Adam. However, this power was usurped by the enemy when Adam and Eve succumbed to the trickery and deception of the enemy.

Recall the instance when Jesus had come out of the wilderness after a 40 day fast and he had the encounter with the devil. The Word of God (Matthew 4) described the devil taking Jesus upon a high mountain and offering him rulership over the kingdoms of the world if He would bow down and worship Him. Of course Jesus did not play into the devil's game. But, what you must understand is that Jesus never denied the fact that the devil was in legal control of these kingdoms. So, when He died on Calvary He went into the underworld and took the authority away from Satan. This legal right and control that was lost in Adam has now been regained in Christ Jesus.

Please have this understanding – just because someone has given you authority does not mean that everyone will honor or respect that authority. This same spirit of disobedience and rebellion runs rampant everywhere from churches, to homes, to communities, to the world at large. There are many who refuse to acknowledge the authority given to those in charge.

Even in your everyday experiences you can see the truth of this point. On the job, there may be a boss or supervisor but everyone does not always submit to the directives of the one in charge. In churches, people have become common with spiritual leadership and do not respect those who have spiritual rule over them as God's Word encourages. In homes, there are children who are willful and disobedient to their own future demise. And it is prevalent in the spirit realm as well. That is why the devil is still *"walking about, seeking whom he may devour".* (I Peter 5:8) Knowing he is already defeated but he is still wasting time trying to deceive others.

The devil does not want to acknowledge his loss of power. He will do everything he can to make you feel powerless and ineffective. This is why he continues to *"steal,*

kill, and destroy" hoping that his actions and antics will discourage you from utilizing the spiritual power (dominion, authority, and control) that has been given to you.

You've had all those sleepless nights and days of unrest wondering what was wrong! You've attended everybody's seminar, read everybody's book, listened to everybody's tape, and quoted every scripture that you can possibly think of. Yet, it still seems as though the enemy is doing everything he can to hinder your every act of faith. Understand that just because you have a title or position doesn't mean that your adversary will respect you. The devil could care less about what church you attend, how long you've been there, what board you serve on or how many other religious activities you engage in. But, God be praised! God has equipped His believers with more than just a title or position.

If you are a believer, then you have *exousia* based upon your covenant relationship with God. There are certain rights and privileges that automatically belong to you when you are born again. Realize that when you experienced the new birth you received a new Father and a new family.

"Wherefore remember, that ye being in time past Gentiles in the flesh, who are called the Uncircumcision in the flesh made by hands; That at that time ye were without Christ, being aliens from the commonwealth of Israel, and

strangers from the covenants of promise, having no hope, and without God in the world: Bt now in Christ Jesus ye who sometimes were far off are made nigh by the blood of Christ." (Ephesians 2:11-13)

Before you came to the Lord, you were "out there!" Whether you did bad things or not, you were outside of the will of God and outside of the blessing of God in regards to your eternal security. But when you received the Lord Jesus Christ as your personal Savior and the Lord of your life, a new relationship with the Father developed. Also, a new relationship with fellow believers was established. Along with these new relationships came new position and authority.

"For as many as are led by the Spirit of God, they are the sons of God. For ye have not received the spirit of bondage again to fear; but ye have received the Spirit of adoption, whereby we cry Abba, Father. The Spirit itself beareth witness with our spirit, that we are the children of God: And if children, then heirs..." (Romans 8:14-17a)

MY BORN AGAIN STATUS
Causes Me To Be Blessed In Relationships With...

GOD ~ MYSELF ~ OTHERS

Yes, your inheritance in the Lord affords you certain rights and privileges. Just because of who you are (and whose you are) there is authority that has been given to you. *Exousia* is the authority, or right or privilege that has been afforded to believers. *Exousia* is good, but God knew that you would need more than just the "legal right" in order to guarantee your victory in the earth realm. He knew that you would not only need power that "says something", but you also would need power that "does something".

The other word – *dunamis* – means special miraculous power. Think of it as the very power of God, because God is the only one who can work a miracle. In the Book of Acts, Chapter 1 and verse 8, the Word of God declares, **"But ye shall receive power..."** This power is not just referring to the right or authority to be effective, but the very ability to accomplish what needs to take place.

Ability Is Potential In Performance!

In grasping a true understanding of the word power, the word ability should be considered. Ability is not just the capacity to accomplish a task, but the actual action required in practice. Ability is potential in performance. How many times have you heard the expression: "talk is cheap"? This expression values action over conversation. Many people get lost in talking about what they can do, will do, should do – but they never do! How amazing and such a waste of time is that type of activity.

A longtime friend of mine, Sis. Irene Johnson Ware, a gospel legend in the radio industry made another adage so popular: "Love is – what love does". That expression encourages you to go beyond mere words in demonstrating what you are saying. If you love someone then your actions should correspond to your profession of love.

Both of these sayings are critical in gaining a better understanding of what ability really is. These basically are saying that ability is not really ability if nothing is accomplished. You have to do something!

You would be very frustrated to purchase an appliance that the salesperson convinced you would meet all of your needs, only to get home and find out that the appliance didn't work. The salesperson's words nor the written guarantee on the box are able to console you. Why? Because you just need the appliance to function. The bottom line is: the appliance is only as good as its performance – not it's potential.

You can talk a good talk but if there is no walk to substantiate the talk – the words are useless. It does not matter that you brag or boast about what you can do. Until you display that you are able to do what you say – you are simply blowing hot air.

Power without performance is not real power. In this respect, power is similar to faith. Look at the following account in the Book of James:

"What doth it profit, my brethren, though a man say he hath faith, and have not works? Can faith save him? If a brother or sister be naked, and destitute of food, And one of you say unto them, Depart in peace, be ye warmed and filled; notwithstanding ye give them not those things which are needful to the body; what doth it profit? Even so faith, if it hath not works, is dead, being alone. Yea, a man may say, Thou hast faith, and I have works: shew me thy faith without thy works, and I will shew thee my faith by my works. Thou believest that there is one God; thou doest well: the devils also believe, and tremble. But wilt thou now, O vain man, that faith without works is dead"? (James 2:14-20)

Power and faith can be interchangeable. Power without action is vain (useless) just like faith without works is dead (useless). In order to activate power, you've got to DO SOMETHING! Stop thinking about it, hoping about it, wondering about it, dreaming about it – JUST DO IT! If you really desire change, if you really want to be blessed, then you must put action with your desires.

The previously mentioned account from the Book of James clearly states that if you don't act out what you believe – then your belief is vain or useless. In the fourteenth verse, the question is asked: *"Can faith save him?"* Since it has been established that faith and power can be interchangeable, ask yourself the question, "Can power save me?" The answer is yes and no.

Why no? Power that is not activated is useless. It is just like having an appliance but no power cord. Or it is like having an appliance that is plugged into the electrical outlet – but someone forgot to pay the power bill. You won't get very much use from that appliance!

The answer is also yes! Power can bring about deliverance, but it (power) must be operable. When the appliance has "juice" or power, then you can accomplish something. When the appliance is connected to the power source it has the energy needed to function at its optimal level.

Yes, when you stay connected to God you can accomplish great things. So many passage verify this. You can do all things through Christ that strengthens you. When you are connected to the true vine, you can ask what you will and it shall be done.

How many times have you wanted results, even prayed for deliverance, but nothing happened? Probably too numerous to tell! Have you ever prayed for a new car, a new job, a husband or a wife, a problem to be solved? You named and claimed, attempted to believe and tried to receive, called and attempted to haul, but still nothing happened! Many have been guilty of not doing what needs to be done in order for change to take place. In order to see your power (faith) in action, ability must be attached to it.

"And in the morning, as they passed by, they saw the fig tree dried up from the roots. And Peter calling to remembrance saith unto Him, Master, behold the fig tree which thou cursedst is withered away. And Jesus answering saith unto them, Have faith in God. For verily I say unto you, That whosoever shall say unto this mountain, Be thou removed, and be thou cast into the sea; and shall not doubt in his heart, but shall believe that those things which he saith shall come to pass, he shall have whatever he saith. Therefore I say unto you, What things soever ye desire,

when ye pray, believe that ye receive them, and ye shall have them." (Mark 11:20-24)

Active Faith Causes Change to Erupt!

Real change will take place only when faith is activated. Mark 11:22 exhorts you to: *"Have faith in God".* Faith and doubt contrast and contradict one another. There is an expression, "If you pray don't worry and if you worry don't pray"! Worry is a symptom (or by-product) of unbelief. And unbelief is a sibling to doubt.

Some have made the statement that faith and doubt cannot co-exist. That is not completely accurate. They can be present at the same time but they will not operate at their ultimate level when the other is present. Your level of reception diminishes when doubt tampers with the airwaves. The more you believe, the more you can receive. However, the more you doubt, the more you hinder what you really need from being made manifest. If the statement: "If you believe, you shall receive" is accurate. Then the converse must also be true: "If you do not believe, then you shall not receive".

This is why you must *"fight the good fight of faith".* Your faith (belief) is under attack. If the devil can keep you from believing then he knows he can succeed in hindering you from receiving. For, if you don't believe that good things can happen for you then you won't look for or expect good things to happen for you. And sometimes blessings will pass right by you because you were not expecting them.

Unbelief Will Hinder Your Harvest

If you continue to the next verse (Mark 11:23), you see the parallel presented in regards to having faith in God. St. Mark says that you have the power or ability to actually move mountains by your heart's belief. If faith (even as a grain of a mustard seed – a very small seed) can move mountains, imagine the size of mountains that can be created by doubt and disbelief. He warns you not to doubt in your heart. When doubt fills a believer's heart, prayers are hindered. This is a reason many people do not reap the harvest they are praying for. They stop believing!

In Ephesians 3:20, the Word of God says that God is able to do **"exceeding abundantly above all that we ask or think, according to the power that worketh in us."** This suggests that oftentimes things are not accomplished in your life because of the lack of power being activated. In this passage translate power to faith or belief or expectation. God is God and He can accomplish great things. However, there are many instances where He is operating based upon the faith you provide. You need to give God something to work with.

Remember the woman with the issue of blood. She had been sick for twelve long years. God knew at the beginning of her sickness that she was ill. And all the time she was running here and there, spending all of her money on different physicians, He knew that she was still ill. When Jesus came to town, He did not advertise that He was looking for her so that she could be healed. But, the Bible plainly states that she began to talk to herself. You need to learn to speak to yourself and encourage yourself to believe God for the miracle that you need.

After she pressed her way through the crowd and touched his garment, the Bible says that she was healed immediately. When Jesus spoke to her, he declared that "her faith" had made her whole. Her miracle was made manifest because of her faith.

I have always considered myself as a water walker. Peter did not stay in the boat with the other disciples when he saw Jesus walking on the water. But, he launched out with faith and got out of the boat and "walked on the water". Yes, when I am trusting and believing God for the miraculous – I give God something to work with: actions that support my unwavering faith. Some have criticized me for doing what seemed to be crazy or even impossible. But, I have always held the conviction that if I am going to trust God, I will do more than just sing about it. I am going to trust Him with my actions. I am not dead yet. So, I still trust God.

God is a multiplier. Go back to math class and multiply anything you want times zero. What is the sum? That's it – zero. Give God something to work with. Extend the faith that has been invested within you to believe for the impossible.

God Is Waiting On You!

Many times things don't happen because power is not activated. That means you have to "do" something. It's unfortunate that some Christians have this "sit back and let God attitude", not realizing that God actually works through people. If you expect God to do anything in the earth realm, you have to also expect Him to use you as a willing vessel.

When things don't happen, it's not because God can't do it, for the Word says He is able to do *"exceedingly abundantly"*. Stop limiting God! When things don't happen, learn to unfold your arms while waiting on God. If His Word declares that He has given you all things that pertain to life and godliness you must begin by activating and releasing the power that should be continuously working in you.

The miraculous working of God that is manifested in your life is in direct proportion to the amount of faith that you release. The Word said according to the power that **worketh** in us. The suffix –eth denotes a continuation of the primary word which is "work". That means that your faith must be a constant and deliberate action and not a sputtering on and off occurrence. When thinking about the deliberateness of one's faith, consider a mighty river. No matter what rocks, valleys or turns are in its path it still flows. Your faith must continue to operate even in the midst of adversity, trials, tribulations and defeat.

Too many give up. Just because you may fail in your attempt that does not mean it is time to call it quits! Sunday morning, the voices resound with the old hymn, "I will trust in the Lord 'till I die". However, observing the actions of some of these same people would cause some to wonder if they have stopped trusting and just died!

On the contrast, in the world there are too many sinners operating in their own brand of "faith"! No, not faith in God!

But the principle of putting action with what their heart and mouth are declaring. When they feel they have a chance to win at gambling they will keep on trying until something happens. There have been people to lose the money in their pockets, the clothes on their backs, and the material possessions they own. Yet, they keep on gambling being driven by a spirit in which they have faith. Oh, if this type "action with belief" was prevalent in the church!

God is not moved by situations. It takes faith to move God. A prime example of how a lack of faith (absence of activated power) hinders a great work is when Jesus attempted ministry in his hometown and the Word of God declares in Mark 6:5 that, **"He could there do no mighty work..."** This was not because Jesus lacked any power or anointing, but because the people were filled with doubt and unbelief. When things don't happen it's not because it's not God's will. Many times people just don't line up with the Word of God (which is God's Will) and blessings are hindered.

Disobedience (unbelief's first cousin) also hinders power from being activated. You must obey the Word of God, the Spirit of God, the Voice of God, and the Move of God if you are to see true deliverance come. A friend of mine has a wonderful message on his answering machine: "If you do it right, God will bless it right". When I first heard it, I smiled. As I began to reflect on it, I realize that it was an awesome message and a great witnessing tool.

Blessings can be forfeited because of disobedience. Remember the incident where Saul disobeyed God and lied to Samuel (I Samuel 15). God told Saul, *"to obey is better than sacrifice."* God gave Saul specific instructions but Saul chose rather to obey his own mind. He even played the blame game and said that it was the people's fault. Don't ever get caught up in the disobedience trap.

So, in actuality, to correctly define power according to the Word of God, power is ability in action. Just like faith without works is dead, so is ability (power) without action dead.

It would be foolish to have a Lexus in the garage and a Mercedes in the driveway and then complain that you don't have transportation. So it is foolish to proclaim that you have power, but you are still living a defeated life. Lack of knowledge can defeat you in your purpose and hinder you in your trek towards destiny. Just as the Word says that a tree is known by the fruit that it bears, so is your power known by your actions.

Whose Power?

Some times people become wrapped up in self and forget about God. This is especially sadly true of people who are gifted and popular among the people. This type attitude and action is quite dangerous. How many times have you heard the phrase, "I am decreasing that God may increase." This statement would be more evident if the order of their actions was changed. It would be much easier to decrease if God was increased in every area of your life.

It's All About Him!

In order to have God increased in your life, He must be your priority and focus of your undivided attention. You must become self-less and put yourself on "ignore". Things that were important to you and your personal agenda must be placed on hold. Your life must be all about Him.

Some years ago, God gave me a revelation regarding "praise and worship", and He shared with me a new order that I coined and began to use at Fellowship Church and abroad as I conducted workshops and seminars. "Praise into Worship" is the correct order. In order to get to worship you must go through praise. Praise is your pursuit of God. And worship is what God allows when you find Him. So, we stopped calling that portion of the service `praise and worship', but we began to call it as it is in practice: "Praise Into Worship".

Order is so very important. The revelation in this shifting is that our ultimate goal is to experience worship with God. Worship is communion, fellowship, intimacy with the Creator. It is all about Him. As the focus moves away from what you are going through, what you are facing, and what is happening to you, then you can experience His presence in such an awesome way.

Speak Into The Atmosphere

So change what you say and sing. Begin to decree and declare. Speak into the atmosphere. Who He is! What He does! And watch what happens. Things around you will begin to change almost immediately. Sickness and infirmity begin to flee. Attitudes and dispositions become positive. Relationships are healed. The mind becomes more receptive to God's Word. All because your focus is on Him and Him alone!

"Submit yourselves therefore to God. Resist the devil, and he will flee from you. Draw nigh to God and he will draw nigh to you..." (James 4:7-8)

Notice the order in the above scripture passage. You must first submit yourself to God; then you will obtain relief from the enemy. You must draw near to God first, and God promises to draw near to you. "Get in order" with God's way and a drastic change will become evident.

Sometimes people get so lost in what is going on around them and "through" them that they forget that the power does not actually belong to them. Be mindful to always remember that you are merely a steward. You don't own anything! Not the clothes on your back, the shoes on your feet, the house in which you live, the car you drive, and especially not the power that flows through you!

I recall a conversation that I had with a gentleman that called himself a prophet. He declared to me that he operated in all nine gifts of the Spirit. I am asked him (out of curiosity) did he have control over when and how the gifts operated. His response was that he was in complete control. My response: I simply smiled.

There was no point arguing or trying to explain that the gifts were God's and not his, and that he really could not just turn them off and on at his will. You have to know when to speak and when to just smile and walk away. It did not matter what I would have said, he was already convinced that he was right and everybody else had much to learn.

Those type people can be quite dangerous. Just know this – God is in control and He is in control alone! He is not sharing His sovereign omnipotence. When God allows His power to be made manifest through His believers, He retains authority over when and how those spiritual gifts will operate. No matter what office you may claim to hold, no matter what anointing you declare to operate under, no matter what power you feel you may have – it all belongs to God. And He decides how His power will be manifest in the earth realm.

It is very tragic to see people who once were so humble and lowly changed by the blessings of God. Can you recall the individual who would come to church every time the church door opened? They would walk, catch a cab, hitch a ride, whatever it took to get there and they were there - and they were on time! Yet, when the blessings of a new car came to them for some strange reason or another, these same people found any and every excuse as to why they could not make it to church!

It is a very dangerous thing to forget who God is and what belongs to Him. Two reminders from the Psalms are found in Psalm 9:17: *"The wicked shall be turned into hell, and all the nations that forget God."* And Psalm 24:1 reminds that, *"The earth is the Lord's and the fulness thereof..."* That means that everything spiritual and natural must answer to God. Everything belongs to God. God is in control!

Man is only a steward. Everything that man has – including ability and potential – comes from God. You simply choose how you use or invest that which the Lord has entrusted unto you. Some are good stewards and some are poor stewards. Even when it comes to power! Good stewards use every available opportunity to allow God to use them. They willingly give of themselves regardless of the personal sacrifice that they may have to make. But, there are others who are cold and stagnant. Poor stewards come up with excuses in refusing to allow God to do anything through them.

Practice Being A Good Steward!

Practice loving people. If you learn to sow into the lives of people, God will take good care of you. But, you must have pure motives. You must love people simply because of God's love that is within you. If you pretend to love people because of the potential reward in the future, you will miss the blessing.

When you come to terms with yourself and admit that by yourself you are nothing, and alone can't accomplish anything – then you will see the miraculous take place. Remember, this "power" belongs to God.

"Daniel answered and said, Blessed be the name of God for ever and ever: for wisdom and might are his: And he changeth the times and seasons: he removeth kings, and setteth up kings: he giveth wisdom unto the wise, and knowledge to them that know understanding: He revealeth the deep and secret things: he knoweth what is in the darkness, and the light dwelleth with him." (Daniel 2:20-22)

The word "might" used here in Daniel 2:20 may also be rendered power. The Hebrew word for might is *gebuwrah*, meaning power; also force, victory, strength.

Here the Word of God clearly shows that power belongs to God. God is truly an awesome God. The power of God is so great that He is the one that ***"changes the times and seasons."*** He even removes and sets up kings. And all this time you thought that things just happened. Not so! Nothing just happens that God does not allow. All spirits are subject to the higher power! The bottom line is everything and everybody must answer to God.

It does not matter if you are a Democrat, Republican, or an Independent. Those are man-made classes that mean very little to God. For, God has a way to operate through all of them for His own glory and purpose.

Not only did Daniel acknowledge that God is the one with power, but David also concurred. In the mouth of these two witnesses, let this point be established. (Matthew 18:16)

David, in his praises unto God, acknowledged that God not only had the legal right, but He had the wherewithal to accomplish whatever He pleased.

"Thine, O Lord, is the greatness, and the power, and the glory, and the victory, and the majesty: for all that is in the heaven and in the earth is Thine; Thine is the kingdom, O Lord, and thou art exalted as head above all. Both riches and honor come of Thee, and Thou reignest over all; and in Thine hand is power and might; and in Thine hand it is to make great, and to give strength unto all." (I Chronicles 29:11-12)

In verse 11, David acknowledges that, *"the greatness, and the power..."* belong to God. He is pointing out that not only is God the owner, but God is also in charge. And in verse 12, he states that, *"in Thine hand is power and might".* In the

Hebrew, the use of the word power is rendered here as *kowach* which literally means force. Figuratively, this same word (*kowach*) is defined as capacity, which means to produce. This is simply saying that God has within His jurisdiction the means to "do or accomplish" what He pleases, when He pleases, and where He pleases. God is sovereign!

Whoever we are and whatever we become is not by our will alone, but because of the mighty working of God's power. The Apostle Paul in his letter to the Ephesians wrote that his ministry was effected, **"according to the gift of the grace of God given unto me by the effectual working of His power".** (Ephesians 3:7). It is the grace of God on your life that enables you to do what you do. That's right, it's not that you have earned or even deserve the right to operate in His power – but His goodness and mercy blesses you to be a blessing. Give God praise for how He decides to use you.

This is not to say that we are mere robots or puppets. God deposits potential within each of us and it is up to us to either activate our faith (which we all have been given) and allow His effectual working power to affect your ministry or you can live in doubt and disbelief. Living in doubt will only allow life to take control of you and prevent you from walking in victory and being in charge of your life.

God Has Invested His Power In His People For His Purpose!

The Word of God admonishes us in Romans 12:3 not to have an exaggerated opinion of our own importance, but rather to rate our ability soberly, according to the degree or level of faith God has given us. Remember, earlier it was discussed about faith and power being interchangeable. So, in light of this understanding, we now understand that it is our job to use the power (ability and authority) God has given us with the understanding that the power is God's and we are His faithful stewards.

Even though the bottom line is that "power" belongs to God, is of God, and is given by God; God is not sitting in heaven holding onto His power. He has given His power to believers through the gift of His Spirit. Yes, the very power of God – He wants to manifest in and through us. Isn't that awesome?

Remember in Matthew 28:18, Jesus said all authority (all power of rule) in heaven and on earth has been given to Me. And in Acts 1:8, the Word declares, **"You shall receive power *(ability, efficiency, and might)* when the Holy Spirit is**

come upon you..." Again, the bottom line is that we are merely stewards. Are you a good steward or a poor steward? Are you faithful or unfaithful? Are you wise or prudent, foolish or careless?

But Ye Shall Receive Power

When the Word of God declares that you shall receive power, it implies that you don't already have "power", or the power that you possess is different from the power being promised. Born again believers should expectantly and purposely seek for the promised power. If God has promised a free gift, you should by all means receive it. Don't let anything or anybody hinder you from being blessed by God.

It Is God's Spirit That Brings You To Salvation!

One thing you must come to terms with (and this of course doesn't fit everybody's doctrine) is the fact that when you received your salvation the Holy Ghost took residence within your heart at that very moment. Yet, there is still a fullness that God wants you to experience. It's almost like you are cooking in the kitchen. Now, very rarely does that aroma just stay in the kitchen, but the aroma (or presence) of that dinner permeates throughout the entire house. That's what God wants to do in your life. He wants to fill every part of you.

Yes, every area of your life needs to be under the influence of the Holy Ghost.

God wants the *exousia* (authority of the believer) to be magnified in you and be expanded to *dunamis* (the force of God) so that you can be a recipient of the **"ye shall receive power"** that was promised in the Book of Acts.

The Power You Receive Is Potent

Some Christians are good people but lack the ingredient for a successful and victorious Christian life – that is power! Not physical power, but spiritual power. Many are crying out for deliverance – but it just won't seem to come. Going to church week after week, paying tithes and giving offerings, singing in the choir and serving on the usher board are all good and right things to do, but these activities in and of themselves are not the real source of power. Real power must come from God because it belongs to God. Consider the words of the prophet Zerubbabel, **"Not by might, nor by power, but by my Spirit, saith the Lord of hosts."** (Zechariah 4:6) The power that you "shall receive" is not a physical power or a power of man's might. It is something much greater – much more potent!

Matthew 28:19 declares, *"All power is given unto me in heaven and in earth."* Jesus made this statement after his defeat of death and the grave. ALL refers not just to power here on earth below, but also power in the heavenlies above. This same ALL POWER is what causes chains to be broken, yokes to be destroyed, the devil to flee, and infirmities to wither away. This is the same ALL POWER that has been promised to believers after the Holy Ghost has come upon them. This is the same ALL POWER that translates you from spiritual death to abundant life and causes you to become the sons of God.

Yes, Jesus promised the disciples that after the Holy Ghost came upon them that they would "receive power". He even alluded to their ability in the Gospel of St. John when he said, *"Verily, verily, I say unto you, He that believeth on me, the works that I do shall he do also; and greater works than these shall he do; because I go unto my Father."* (John 14:12) This prophetically spoke of the age of the Holy Spirit when believers would be endued with power to accomplish the impossible. Care must be taken to remember that Jesus desires his ministry to be magnified. When you receive the Spirit of God and begin to allow His Spirit to work the works - that magnification takes place! **The day of the Holy Spirit is here—and it's time for you to receive the Spirit of God so He can do the miraculous through you!**

Understanding mechanically that power is potential in action, you must also understand what power is scripturally and spiritually. The power referred to in this portion of Scripture is *dunamis* "the very ability of God." That's right, God has invested a power in you that when it is activated: His ability invades your situation. He steps into your madness. He gets involved with your circumstance.

Who and What You Are Have Nothing To Do With God's Power Working Through You!

Of course, the disciples felt that they could not have the very ability of God because they were mere men. However, Jesus promised them that they would receive miraculous ability after the Holy Ghost came upon them. In the Gospel of St. John 7:37 Jesus declared, *"If any man thirst, let him come* unto me, and drink. He that believeth on me, as the scripture hath said, out of his belly shall flow rivers of living water."

"**Rivers of living water?**" Well in verse 39, the Word of God takes away any temptation to misinterpret or describe this as something else. But the Bible plainly declares, *"But this spake He of the Spirit, which they that believe on Him should receive...."* These rivers signify a mighty force or power. And of course when the Holy Ghost made his appearance on the Day of Pentecost, he did so with a mighty force and power.

"And when the day of Pentecost was fully come, they were all with one accord in one place. And suddenly there came a sound from heaven as of a rushing mighty wind, and it filled all the house where they were sitting. And there appeared unto them cloven tongues like as of fire, and it sat upon each of them. And they were all filled with the Holy Ghost , and began to speak with other tongues, as the Spirit gave them utterance."
(Acts 2: 1-4)

Not only are the rivers important, but the "living water" should be understood. Water is a necessary ingredient in the sustenance of physical life, but living water is necessary for maintenance of a spiritual life. It is so necessary that Paul urged the Ephesians to *"be filled with the Spirit."* This is not a once-in-a-lifetime event but a daily occurrence. It should be continual. Every day true believers should desire to be filled over and over with the Spirit of God. Understand that when the rivers of the Holy Ghost fill your life, change must erupt. The power of these rivers cleanses and purifies the believer. Just as a natural river channels its way through rocks, limbs, and anything else that would attempt to hinder it—so is the Holy Ghost in a believer's life. The things that used to hinder you, slow you down, or defeat you—can no longer overpower you because of the rivers of living water that you possess.

Now, what about this being "filled" with the Spirit of God? Visualize a man sitting next to a river. The man is thirsty so he leans over and drinks water from the river. Is he "filled"? Technically speaking, no! Even if he drinks a great amount, he is still not "filled". Yet, the river from which he drank is now a part of him. Let's take this same man and place him in the river. No, not waist deep. Place him on the bottom of the river. How much water do you suppose would he consume (or would consume him)?

That same picture is what God wants to do with you. Do not be satisfied with simply coming unto Jesus, meeting Him and then leaving going on your way without allowing Him to bring to full maturity all He desires to do within you. God wants the rivers of the Holy Ghost to consume every area of your spirit, soul, and body. Just like the man at the bottom the river, God wants you to die to sin, the flesh, and self, and then learn to live unto Him.

The Baptism In The Holy Ghost Is Still Relevant Today

The Baptism in the Holy Ghost is a necessary part of every powerful believer's life. For this experience is the same experience that occurred in the disciples' and others' lives all through the Book of Acts. It is still relevant today. Do not let anyone deceive you and tell you that it was only for the early church.

The Baptism of Power is for everyone who desires to experience the fullness of God's Spirit in their life. Do not settle for a "business as usual" mentality or lifestyle. Determine within yourself to receive all that God has for you!

You Can Be Baptized In The Holy Ghost Right Now, At This Very Moment!

If you think you have power now, accept the challenge to allow the rivers to flow in your life. If you think you're a great prayer warrior, teacher of the Word, witness or child of God—you would be pleasantly surprised after experiencing the Baptism in the Holy Ghost.

Yes whoever you are and whatever you are doing will be magnified. It will be magnified because you have a new power source operating in you. And as you continue to do kingdom work in the earth realm – you will discover a fresh and powerful presence that you never experienced before.

Receiving this power is neither a difficult nor a time consuming process. What must be present is "faith and action." First, believe and then receive! If you simply trust God, He will fill you with His Spirit even now. You don't have to be in the sanctuary of a church or even have the presence of others to experience the fullness of God's Spirit in your life.

One truth about humanity that many people fail to consider in ministry is that God is the only constant! God is God and He nor His Word changes. But, we as humans are all different. We are different from each other and as we live our lives we find ourselves different from our own selves. Think about it! You are not the same person you used to be ten or twenty years ago. Your exposure to and revelation of God's Word has made changes in you. Your life experiences (including situations, circumstances and conditions) have changed you. Some things have made you bitter. And some things have made you better.

And because you are different – don't always expect to experience God exactly like someone else. Learn to be sensitive to God's Spirit and discover the best practice for you in receiving all that God is doing. Those who believe that they need to wait at the altar for God's presence are no better or worse than those who believe that they can simply pray and ask God for His presence and power and receive it.

Seven Keys To Receiving The Baptism In The Holy Ghost!

There is no specific formula for receiving the Baptism in the Holy Ghost. It is simply a free gift for believers. So, if you are a believer you must simply exercise your faith to receive what God has already given. Following are seven keys to receiving the Baptism in the Holy Ghost:

- Salvation is the only prerequisite (John 7:37, Acts 2:37-38)
- Know that the Spirit is already given (Acts 2, Acts 19, Acts 8: 14-17)
- Don't fear receiving something false (Luke 11: 11-13)
- Don't allow spectators to confuse (Acts 10:44, Romans 8:26, Jude 20)
- Receive upon the laying of hands (Acts 8: 17-19, Acts 19:6)
- Open your mouth (Job 29:21-23, John 7: 37-39)
- Speak as the Spirit gives utterance (Acts 2:4, Acts 10:46, Acts 19:6)

When Jesus promised the disciples that they would receive power when the Holy Ghost came upon them, He literally meant that they would be changed to the extent that a new force, a new energy, a new Spirit would influence them in such a way that they would begin to make a real impact in Jerusalem, Judea, Samaria and all across the globe. Yes, there is a power that God wants you to receive. The very power of God! The Spirit of God! For this power will not only change your life, but will bless countless others.

You should be excited about receiving a gift from God. You should be especially excited about receiving this gift realizing the potential of what it can do in your home, on your job, in your neighborhood, in your church and even in your personal life.

From Whence Cometh this Power?

"The wind bloweth where it listeth, and thou hearest the sound thereof, but canst not tell whence it cometh, and whither it goeth: so is everyone that is born of the Spirit." John 3:8

Some believers allow religion to control them and fail to realize that what they search futilely for on the outside is already within them. For a clearer understanding of this principle, take a closer look at Acts 1:8.: *"But ye shall receive power, after that the Holy Ghost is come UP on you..."*

The Word of God says that you would receive power after the Holy Ghost is come "UPon" you. For something to come "UP—on" you, it must first be "DOWN – in" you! Now, this is a truth that has divided many people who have doctrinal differences. But, the Word of God (not some denominational teaching or man-made tradition) should be the final word in this debate. In order to have a complete understanding of this statement, some sacred cows have to be destroyed.

Point One: Acknowledge the important role of the Holy Ghost in the process of salvation. It is the Spirit of God that brings conviction and draws us to God. In John 16:8, the Bible says, *"And when He is come, He will reprove the world*

of sin......" When the Bible says that the Spirit of God will "reprove" the world, it means to bring under conviction. The Greek word for reprove is *elegcho*. This means to convince, refute, expose, or bring to shame the person being reproved. One of the Holy Spirit's job descriptions is to identify error and then lead and guide into truth! (John 16:13)

The Spirit of God is the agent by which the new birth occurs. In order to be a Christian, you must be born of the Spirit. You must undergo a spiritual birth. Religion offers a natural new birth, but God said it must be spiritual.

"Jesus answered and said unto him, verily, verily, I say unto thee, Except a man be born again, he cannot see the kingdom of God. Nicodemus saith unto him, How can a man be born when he is old? Can he enter the second time into his mother's womb, and be born? Jesus answered, Verily, verily, I say unto thee, Except a man be born of water and of the Spirit, he cannot enter into the kingdom of God. That which is born of the flesh is flesh; and that which is born of the Spirit is spirit. Marvel not that I said unto thee, ye must be born again." (John 3:3-7)

It is not good enough to try and stop doing bad things and start doing good things in order to get right with God. That is a flesh operation and not spiritual. In order to enter into and maintain the covenant relationship with God that you need and desire, you must trust His Word and be dependent upon His Spirit. The new birth must begin on the inside. Being born again is not dictated by the clothes you wear on the outside, but it is realized when true change occurs on the inside.

Point Two: Understand that when a person is saved (born again), the Spirit of God takes residence at that very moment! Okay, those of you who have been taught differently, please continue breathing. Let the Word of God make itself plain unto you.

"So then they that are in the flesh cannot please God. But ye are not in the flesh, but in the Spirit, if so be that the Spirit of God dwell in you. Now if any man have not the Spirit of Christ, he is none of his. And if Christ be in you, the body is dead because of sin; but the Spirit is life because of righteousness. But if the Spirit of him that raised up Jesus from the dead dwell in you, he that raised up Christ from the dead shall also quicken your mortal bodies by his Spirit that dwelleth in you." (Romans 8: 8-11)

Now that was a mouthful, wasn't it! Yet, it is so simple! Either you have God's Spirit and you belong to Him, or you don't have His Spirit and you don't belong to Him. When a person accepts Jesus Christ as their Lord and Saviour, at that very moment they become a child of God. If they are a child of God, then they must have His Spirit.

Water, Tongues, Or Blood?

This eliminates the teaching and presumption by some that you have to "speak in tongues" to be saved. If baptism (either water or spirit) is the agent of salvation, what was the purpose of the blood that was shed on Calvary? Read Ephesians 2:13, **"But now in Christ Jesus ye who sometimes were far off are made nigh by the blood of Christ."** It was His blood that signed the adoption papers to bring you into the family of God. It was God's Spirit that persuaded you and brought you to the point of accepting His grace that was extended unto you.

Feelings, emotions, signs, wonders, or any other exterior manifestations have nothing to do with the fact that the person is born again (by the Spirit of God). You must simply just believe God's Word. If God said you belong to Him and you have His Spirit, then it is your responsibility to learn what God has invested within you. Now, of course this still just doesn't sit well with some. The bottom line is this: What does it take to get saved? Speaking in tongues doesn't save. Abstinence from bad habits doesn't save. Water baptism doesn't save. Going to church and doing good works doesn't save. **But BLOOD DOES!** We are saved by grace through faith in the shed blood of Jesus Christ. It's a faith thing! And if it is done by faith, then we must acknowledge that faith is equivalent to the Word. Faith does come by hearing the Word, right? And Jesus Christ is the Word in the flesh, is that correct? And the Word, the Father and the Holy Spirit are one, right? Then the Spirit must be the agent by which we are saved and kept. Now everything else that the Spirit does after that fact is secondary: the tongues, the gifts, the ministries, etc.

Point Three: In regards to the fullness of the Spirit (or Baptism in the Holy Ghost), learn how to call up and out that which has been invested down and within. This is where you must again just obey the Word of God. Stop looking for something to fall out of the sky, flow through the preacher's hand and knock you off your feet! Rather, look for the Spirit of God that God said was within you to begin to flow through whatever else is present within you—cleansing you, filling you, renewing you, restoring you, refreshing you, purging you, healing you, etc. In John 5:7, the Word of God says that there are three that bear record in heaven: the Father, the Word and the Holy Ghost, and these three are one. If the Bible says they are one, then who are we to contradict God's Word? One is one. And one means the same.

To help you with a definite understanding of what role the Holy Ghost has in a born again individual's life, you need to understand the Godhead- Father, Son, and Holy Ghost. The best way to understand God in His completeness is to understand Him in creation. In Genesis 1:26 God said, **Let US make man in OUR IMAGE.** That means, when God made man, He made him similar (or in His own likeness) to Himself. Well, in order to understand the spiritual first get a grip on the natural. **"Howbeit that was not first which is spiritual, but that which is natural; and afterward that which is spiritual."** (I Corinthians 15:46)

You And God Are Triune: Spirit – Soul – Body

Man is a three-part being. In his purest essence he is a spirit being. He possesses a soul (emotions, mind, will, intellect, and desires). And all of this is housed in his body (flesh, outermost man). Now, when God created man, if He did this in His image we must conclude that God is also three-part (Father, Son, and Holy Ghost). Just one GOD! Not three Gods, but ONE with three parts! John 4:24 says that **"God is a spirit..."** That is the purest and truest essence of God. God is a spirit. But God is much more than just Spirit, for there are two more parts. God also has a body.

In the beginning was the Word, and the Word was with God, and the Word was God. The same was in the beginning with God. All things were made by him; and without him was not anything made that was made, In him was life; and the life was the light of men. And the light shineth in darkness; and the darkness comprehended it not. And the Word was made flesh, and dwelt among us (and we behold his glory, the glory as of the only begotten of the Father), full of grace and truth. (John 1:1-5,14)

Jesus Christ, the Son of God, God Himself, **"Who, being in the form of God, thought it not robbery to be equal with God,"** (Philippians 2:6) Also, we must note that in Colossians 2:9, the Word of God further informs us that, **"In Him (Christ Jesus) dwelleth all the fullness of the Godhead bodily."** The final part of the Godhead – The Spirit of God (Ephesians 4:30), prays and groans (Romans 8:26, 27), loves (Romans 15:30). When a sinner comes to the Lord and is born-again, something wonderful and miraculous takes place. According to God's Word in I Corinthians 5:18, **"Old things are passed away, and behold, all things are new."** This means that this individual has been changed to the extent that there is a "newness" within Him. The Word of God says that no man is Christ's unless he has the Spirit of Christ (Romans 8:9).

With this information, break down those sacred cows of salvation and the Holy Ghost. Believe God's Word and do not allow the tradition of man to fill your heart and mind. Don't buy into the misconception that unless you have spoken in tongues that you aren't really saved.

According to the Word of God, the Holy Ghost enters a person the moment they are born again. But understand, that does not mean that God does not want to do more in them. For the Baptism in the Holy Ghost is a real and important part of every believer's life. It is a distinct experience that follows the new birth.

The Bible even encourages you to receive the baptism when Jesus stood and cried, saying, ***"He that believeth on me, as the scripture hath said, out of his belly (innermost thing) shall flow rivers of living water. (But spake He of the Spirit, which they believe on him should receive: for the Holy Ghost was not yet given; because that Jesus was not yet glorified).*** (John 7: 38, 39)

Well, there is good news for you—Jesus has been glorified and the Holy Ghost has been given! That means that not only can you have joy in knowing that the Spirit of God dwells in you, but your joy can be full in releasing the gift of God by allowing the rivers of living water to flow out of your innermost being.

Yes, the waters of the Holy Ghost will flow out of you! A statement that I have often times made is: **"The power is not in the pulpit—but it's in the pew!"** There are rivers on the inside of you, waiting to burst forth and completely engulf every area of your life!

Where's the Power?

There used to be a television commercial that asked the question—"Where's the beef?" Today, we are presented with another question—**Where's the Power?**" THE POWER OF GOD! In regards to the power of God, do not be deceived. *"Now concerning spiritual gifts, brethren, I would not have you ignorant."* (I Corinthians 12:1)

God does not want His power to be some great mystery for His children. He wants His children to be knowledgeable about the spiritual resources that are available for them. When the scriptures declare that people are destroyed for a lack of knowledge, it is this type lack that causes spiritual ruin and decay in the lives of people. Not knowing what is available and how to access it can yield a life of barrenness and impotence.

The power of God has been invested in the church of God. And the church of God is made manifest through the people of God. This does not mean that God's power is reserved for some elite few in leadership. God's power most definitely is not intended for people operating for their own purpose or agenda. And do not be deceived by counterfeit people who actually are exhibiting a resemblance of power which really is not power at all.

The Power Is In The Pew

First and foremost, all of God's power is not in the heavenlies. God has not limited His power to only be in the throne room in heavens above. When Jesus conquered hell, death and the grave He boldly declared that all power in heaven and earth is given unto me. And then shortly thereafter, He declared how through the Spirit of God His power would be shared with believers all over the world. By the same token, His power is not reserved only for the pulpit. The power of God is also **in the pew**.

"Now there are diversities of gifts, but the same Spirit. And there are differences of administrations, but the same Lord. And are diversities of operations, but it is the same God which worketh all in all. But the manifestation of the Spirit is given to every man to profit withal." (I Corinthians 12:4-7)

You cannot be afraid to be used of God. When the enemy tries to remind you of your flesh challenges – agree with him and tell him that you are an imperfect vessel that God decided to use for His glory and His purpose. That's God's way. He uses the very people that others discount and write off.

Thank God for Rahab, the harlot, hiding and protecting the spies. Praise God for Balaam's ass (even though he was just an animal) who was used to speak to a hard headed servant. Moses and David both were murderers but God still used them to bless His people. Hallelujah even for me! I decree and declare every Sunday that I am anointed by God for His purpose but that does not mean I do not have challenges with my flesh suit. I am thankful that God does not change His mind about his gifts and callings. He uses me in spite of my own silly self!

I get excited talking to people who are not regular church goers. For some strange reason they have been made to feel like there is no place in the church for them. But, these are some of the very people that God wants to use. He wants people who are real. People who don't wear masks and do not mind being transparent are blessings in God's work. God is not glorified by people masquerading and parading in the sanctuary as they are the only ones with a direct connection to the Father.

The gift of power is for all – Not just a select few!

The Word of God says that every man has been given the manifestation of the Spirit. God is revealing Himself to mankind. God is moving across the man made barriers of race, culture, and denominations to fulfill the Word of God as prophesied in the Book of Joel. People everywhere and from every walk of life are experiencing the manifestation of the Spirit of God.

"And it shall come to pass afterward, that I will pour out my spirit upon all flesh; and your sons and your daughters shall prophesy, your old men shall dream dreams, your young men shall see visions. And also upon the servants and upon the handmaids in those days will I pour out my spirit. (Joel 2: 28-29)

The outpouring of God's spirit is not reserved for a particular denomination. God will manifest wherever there are people who will welcome His presence and believe in His power. You will find Baptist believers, Catholic believers, Methodist believers, Pentecostal believers, and Presbyterian and Lutheran believers all reaching out to God in varied ways.

Stop trying to box in the Spirit of God. Because humanity is multi-faceted and varied, it is no surprise that there are differences in how people respond to the Spirit of God. You cannot make people "do what you do" in order to prove that they have the Spirit of God in manifestation.

I have been to churches where those who were in ministry seemed to try and force others to speak in tongues in order to "receive" the power of God. If you have to force someone to speak in another tongue, I question the validity of that tongue. I have always been of the persuasion that the Baptism in the Holy Ghost is just like a lace-up shoe. The tongues are just there! You don't have to look for them or struggle for them. They are just there. But, the power of God is much more than people speaking in a language they have never learned.

Now, that God is revealing Himself, it is up to you to **do something** with what God is showing you. There are men, women, boys, and girls all across the globe operating under the anointing of God. God is doing His part, and it is up to you to accept this free gift (the gift of power) and walk in the victory and the power promised in the Book of Joel.

Many believers don't realize that they have power. They walk in defeat because they feel that all of the power is in the pulpit or in someone else. This type attitude limits what can take place in a person's life—because what that person can receive is limited by their concept of someone being more qualified. This type of low self-esteem and attitude of personal ineffectiveness is much too prevalent in the church today! There are people who feel that because of their spiritual development (or lack thereof), emotional stability or physical condition—that someone else is better suited to be used of God. I disagree! God uses whom He pleases.

There is a passage of scripture found in Romans 12:3 that states, **"For I say through the grace given unto me, to every man that is among you, not to think of himself more highly that he ought to think; but to think soberly, according as God hath dealt to every man the measure of faith."** If you look at this scripture carefully—it never says not to think highly of oneself (or not to have a balanced level of self-confidence and self-worth), but it dictates not to think "more highly than he ought to think."

A certain level of confidence, worthiness, ego is healthy. Without these productive ingredients faith is impossible. For faith has to *"call those things that be not as though they were."* When someone can believe the unbelievable, see the invisible, touch the intangible and achieve the impossible then that person is ready to flow in the power of God.

Many people don't experience the manifestation of the power of God because they are focused on an individual and not on God. Some people miss out because of giving God's glory to a man or woman. God is not willing to share His glory with anyone! In Isaiah 42:8, He said, *"I am the Lord: that is my name: and my glory will I not give to another, neither my praise to graven images."*

This is a very common problem: people being hooked on personalities and not on Jesus. It is foolish to debate over whether you are a follower of Paul or a follower of Apollos. Salvation resides in neither one of them. I love to listen to T.D Jakes and Rod Parsley. I respect the ministries of Benny Hinn and Gloria Copeland. I admire the teachings of Creflo Dollar and Fred Price. And, I'm just crazy about the fervor and intensity of Paula White and Jamal Bryant. BUT! They are all just men and women who God has anointed for a season and a purpose. There is no salvation, no deliverance, no prosperity, no power in any of them! God is not sharing His glory with any mortal man!

Another example of how people "miss" God is when they feel like if a particular person can't do it—it can't be done! Well, unless that person is God—they are sadly mistaken.

Man Can't Save You!

I recall a young man that I had been pleading with to give his life to God. Well, his response was "I'm going to let my pastor save me". Two problems: One his pastor didn't have the power to save him (only God can). Two, his pastor died! Now, this young man is still lost, still outside of the will of God—and all I can do is continue to pray that he will yield before his time runs out!

Other people miss out on the manifestation of God's power because of a lack of faith. It takes faith to receive anything from God. Hebrews 11:6 declares **"But without faith it is impossible to please Him: for he that cometh to God must believe that he is, and that he is a rewarder of them that diligently seek Him."** God is not moved by your situation—it takes faith to move God!

There are people who live here in the United States and attend church on a regular basis and have never experienced a miracle of God. Yet, there are many in third World countries that hear the Gospel, believe the Gospel, and experience miracles. Why? Because of faith! It's so strange that people who supposedly know God have trouble in receiving the manifestation of God.

Again, the power is not in the pulpit. Many people have focused their eyes on man and not on God. There is another problem with this—God is constant, man is "sometimey". Just because someone wears a title or delivers a message does not validate them.

But there were false prophets, also among the people, even as there shall be false teachers among you, who privily shall bring upon themselves swift destruction. And many shall follow their pernicious(destructive) ways; by reason of whom the way of truth shall be evil spoken of. And through covetousness shall they with the feigned(deceptive) words make merchandise of you: whose judgement now of a long time lingereth not, and their damnation slumbereth not. (II Peter 2: 1-3)

Look Out For The Wolves
Dressed In Sheep Clothing!

The world is full of people who purposely deceive and manipulate others. They appear to be holy and full of power when in essence they are unholy and filled with wickedness. It is sad to see so many gullible people being deceived and led astray. It seems as though their spiritual vision has been hindered. Even though, Satan has transformed himself into an "angel of light", still it seems as though some of these people would wake up and smell the coffee! Basically, you have wolves dressed in sheep clothing that fill pulpits, broadcast on television and radio, and hold meetings from town to town.

I am so tired of every week a new prophet shows up or a new traveling evangelist is in town. Don't get me wrong, there are legitimate men and women of God that God uses to go here and there to do His bidding. But, just like God has true representatives the devil also has people who are working in his camp. You must have spiritual discernment to know who these people are. They all show up with the same pitch: "You need to meet me at the meeting!" Aren't you tired of meeting man? Aren't you tired of meeting flesh? It's time for God's people to meet God and realize the real "power" of God that will flow through regular ordinary people like you and me!

Colossians warns you to **"Beware lest any man spoil you through philosophy and vain deceit, after the tradition**

of men, after the rudiments of the world, and not after Christ." (Colossians 2:8)

The Word of God says that these people shall secretly bring in destructive heresies. Heresies are opinions and beliefs which are contrary to sound Biblical doctrine. Not only will they bring in opinions and beliefs that are in error, but the Word of God says that they will also deny their Redeemer— who is Jesus Christ. The power is NOT in these individuals. Yet, they cause many people to be swayed, moved and ultimately deceived.

I recall a conversation with my father. I asked him how evil and ungodly people had people who were willing to follow them and engage in sinful and sometimes humanely atrocious practices. And his answer was simple but profound. He said, "All leaders will have followers." After thinking about that it made so much sense. Just because you have leadership skills and can sway people to what you are saying or doing does not mean that you are called or anointed by God.

Be careful of anyone who shines the light on themselves and not on Christ. These type people have crept into the church and made themselves quite comfortable. And some people are so gullible that they will believe any and everything that comes off the lips of polished speakers. Guard your heart and mind against such foolishness.

Power in Practice

If real power is the very ability of God, then you must admit that when God moves "something happens". Take for example the instance in the Gospel of St. Luke where Jesus healed the child of a man in the crowd, the power of God is clearly seen. When Jesus rebuked the unclean spirit, healed the child, and delivered him again to his father, the Bible says that the people "were all amazed at the mighty power of God". When the power of God is manifested—"something happens"!

I can recall a particular service at Fellowship Church in Mobile, Alabama where God showed up in such an awesome way. There was a young man who walked with a limp. He used either a wheelchair or crutches to get around. One of his legs was shorter than the other. This particular service the power of God was manifest to such an extent you could just "feel Jesus" all in the room. During the ministry period, hands were laid on him and we all saw the miracle. His leg stretched. Yes, in that service God's power stretched that man's leg and he walked out without the assistance of crutches, a wheelchair or anyone else. This is a prime example of how God can "show up and show out".

Ability is Potential In Performance

In understanding the Greek term *dunamis*, the word ability may be applied. In this instance, ability is not just the capacity to accomplish a task—but the wherewithal to see the task completed. Ability is potential in performance. Thus, power is taking a situation and effecting change. Power without performance is not real power! In this respect, power is quite similar to faith.

If you claim to have "power", then you must activate and use or demonstrate the "power" you claim to possess. Too many believers "talk a good talk" but their walk just doesn't line up. There are too many situations where Christians are losing battles to the enemy! It does not matter what it looks like or feels like, you must be committed to standing on God's Word. His Word is truth.

The facts may say one thing, but as a believer you can make the facts change by exercising your faith and trusting God's Word. God's Word will not and cannot fail. You cannot give up in the middle of the battle. You have to learn to endure to the end – especially since God already told you that you were the victor.

Even though, sometimes it may seem as if you are under constant attack, simply use the defensive and offensive weapons that God has given—and you would be amazed at the results. Don't just sit back and allow circumstances and situations to rule your life. Take (even by force) what God says belongs to you! Your peace, your joy, your faith are not negotiable – they are yours and you must refuse to bend to the antics of the enemy.

I'm A Soldier, In The Army Of The Lord!

God's Word is a weapon. Your praise is a weapon. Your faith is a weapon. The armor of God found in the Book of Ephesians is a weapon. If you want to win the fight – use the weapons that God has equipped you.

We are in a constant warfare! The devil is doing all He can to deceive you into defeat. He knows He can't win because victory already belongs to you. But, if he can convince you to stop fighting then he knows you will forfeit the fight. Don't just let the praise team sing: "I'm a soldier, in the army of the Lord". But, live it everyday!

The power of God is not some mystical force to be used only in case of emergency. It's not to be a last resort (like prayer is for some people). It's not to be a last ditch effort in a struggle to obtain a desire or result. But, the power of God is at your disposal to be used every waking moment of the day.

What doth it profit, my brethren, though a man say he hath faith(power), and have not works(actions)?can faith(power) save him? If a brother or sister be naked, and destitute of daily food, And one of you say unto them, Depart in peace, be ye warmed and filled; notwithstanding ye give them not those things which are needful to the body; what doth it profit? Even so faith, if it hath not works, is dead, being alone. Yea, a man may say, Thou hast faith, and I have works: show me thy faith without thy works, and I will show thee my faith by my works. Thou believest that there is one God; thou doest well : the devils also believe, and tremble. But wilt thou know, O vain man, that faith without works is dead? (James 2: 14-20)

Power without action is dead power. What good is it to have an appliance that is top of the line—state of the art and it can't do what it claims? You might as well not have it. So it is with power that doesn't work—you might as well not have it.

It's time that the "power" of God is evident in all believers. Remember, Mark 16:17 did say that *"these signs shall follow them that believe."* It's time for the believers to stop following signs and begin to line up with the Word of God. The signs should be following the believers! God is looking for a church of power:

Not a choir that only sings about it!
Not a preacher that just preaches about it!
Not a people that just shout about it!

The time is over for churches and believers operating out of the will of God! Jesus told the disciples to heal the sick, raise the dead, and cast out devils. And in many churches just the opposite is taking place: they are casting out the sick, praying for the dead, and raising the devil! But, God is looking for a people who desire to manifest His presence! He wants to show up in ordinary people just like you and begin doing the miraculous. *"But we have this treasure in earthen vessels, that the excellency of the power may be of God, and not of us."* (II Corinthians 4:7)

What is this "treasure" in earthen vessels that God has invested in you? This treasure is power, not just *exousia*, but *dunamis*—the very ability of God! Mountain moving ability!

Devil defeating ability! Sickness healing ability! Victorious living ability!

The beauty about this power in you is that God knowingly and willingly invested this awesomeness in imperfect people. God's love for you superseded your faults and failures. That is another trick of the enemy. If the devil can make you think you are not "good enough" for God's power to move through you then you won't believe it will nor will you operate in it. Because the enemy knows your potential he does what he can to discourage you from utilizing the investment that God made in you.

God Invested His Power In Imperfect Vessels Of Clay

Now, there is something you must understand about this "ability" or this power. Real power is made more powerful when it is under pressure or under stress.

"We are troubled on every side, yet not distressed; we are perplexed, but not in despair; Persecuted, but not forsaken; cast down, but not destroyed; Always bearing about in the body in the dying of the Lord Jesus, that the life also of Jesus

might be made manifest in our body." (II Corinthians 4: 8-10)

Yes, sometimes in life you may be troubled or unsettled, you may be perplexed or confused, you may be persecuted and cast down—but you do not have to be stressed out, don't be in despair (without hope), don't be forsaken, and definitely do not stress over being destroyed. You must understand that through your relationship with Jesus Christ you have identified with Him. You not only identify with His death, but also with His life. According to the above scripture, the life of Jesus is to be made manifest in your body. What was the life of Jesus?

"And there was delivered unto him the book of the prophet Esaias. And when he had opened the book, he found the place where it was written, The Spirit of the Lord is upon me, because he hath anointed me to preach the gospel to the poor; he hath sent me to heal the brokenhearted, to preach deliverance to the captives, and recovering of sight to the blind, to set at liberty them that are bruised, To preach to the acceptable year of the Lord. And he closed the book, and he gave it again to the minister, and sat down. And the eyes of all them that were in the synagogue were fastened on him. And he began to say unto them, This day is the scripture fulfilled in your ears. And all bare him witness,

and wondered at the gracious words which proceeded out of his mouth. And they said, Is not this Joseph's son? And he said unto them, Ye will surely say unto me this proverb, Physician, heal thyself: whatsoever we have heard done in Capernaum, do also here in thy country. And he said, Verily I say unto you, No prophet is accepted in his own country. But I tell you of a truth, many widows were in Israel in the days of Elias, when the heaven was shut up three years and six months, when great famine was throughout all the land; But unto none of them was Elias sent, save unto Sarepta, a city of Sidon, unto a woman that was a widow. And many lepers were in Israel in the time of Eliseus the prophet; and none of them was cleansed, saving Naaman the Syrian. And they filled the synagogue, when they heard these things, were filled with wrath, And rose up, and thrust him out of the city, and led him unto the brow of the hill whereon their city was built, that they might cast him down headlong. But he passing through the midst of them went his way, And came down to Capernaum, a city of Galilee, and taught them on the Sabbath days. And they were astonished at his doctrine: for his word was with power." (Luke 4:17-32)

Oh, how awesome! Take out your Holy Ghost mirror and see yourself in this portion of Scripture. That's what Jesus did. He opened the Book of Isaiah and showed himself to the people. You must do the same thing. Yes, you have to open the Word of God and show yourself to the people. Just be certain that when you "show yourself" to the people—that they see the Word of God shining through you and not the "you" whom you used to be.

Even though you are not perfect, your walk and testimony before others should be one that glorifies God and is encouraging to others. You need to be real enough that people can identify with you. But, you must be different enough to be an example and a role model for others. At Fellowship Church our church slogan is: "A Perfecting Place For Imperfect People." Each week we remind each other and inform visitors that none of us have arrived. In the words of my wife, "None of us have ascended." Everybody has issues. But at the same time, we are mindful to not glory in our imperfection and at the same time not to be ashamed of who and what we are because it gives hope to others.

"Verily, verily, I say unto you, He that believeth on me, the works that I do shall he do also; and greater works that these shall he do; because I go unto my Father." (John 14:12)

You must realize who you are in Christ Jesus. God has anointed you to preach good news to the poor, heal those whose hearts have been broken, and to preach deliverance to those who have been bound and made captives of sin, sickness, and death. God has also anointed you to preach and minister the restoration of physical and spiritual sight to the blind, and to free those who have been bound and oppressed by the adversities of life.

You don't need a "title" to operate in this anointing! You don't have to have a robe or stand in a pulpit. All you have to do is be willing and obedient. God is looking for people who are willing to "do the work of the ministry" and not just talk about it. God's anointing does not have to be validated by man. You do not have to be a people pleaser. Strive to please God. Be comfortable with who you are in Christ and with what He has assigned for you to accomplish in the earth realm.

Now, of course there is a price tag that comes with this anointing. But, God has equipped you to stand anyhow! There are those who will be angry and upset with you. For many reasons of course: 1) because of who you are (or more directly who they knew you to be [the old you]), 2) because this power may make them uncomfortable (because of sin in their life or even jealousy), and 3) because the truth you speak may not line up with their traditional beliefs or dogma.

In the midst of this wrath and indignation against you, people may put you out, shut you out, close you out or even try and run you out. But, just realize in the midst of whatever you go through for the gospel's sake, the life of Jesus is just "showing up" in you!

More Power

"Wherefore I put thee in remembrance that thou stir up the gift of God, which is in thee by putting on of my hands. For God hath not given us the spirit of fear, but of power, and of love, and of a sound mind." **II Timothy 1:6-7**

More? A simple definition is: in addition to whatever is already present. "More" also implies that whatever is present is insufficient or inadequate to meet present or future needs. More means that I don't have enough. More indicates that lack is present.

Why is it that believers feel the need to search for "more" power? This type of search is no more than a deception and a distraction. The devil's desire is to hinder the will of God and to handicap the efforts of the church. But, God has called us to be knowledgeable (not ignorant) of the devil's tactics and devices. *"Lest Satan should get an advantage of us: for we are not ignorant of his devices."* (II Corinthians 2:11)

This search for power is just one of the many devices of Satan. Remember the mind is a battleground. If he (Satan) can control your thoughts or cause you to think negatively, he succeeds in his objective to *"steal, kill, and destroy"*. (John 10:10)

What better way to keep you from succeeding than to make you believe that you can't succeed. As long as you doubt your ability to progress and do great exploits—you won't even attempt them. This is why Paul informed Timothy, that God did not give him the spirit of fear. When you recognize and distinguish the spirits operating around you, and engage in effective spiritual warfare against them—then you will be able to walk in real victory.

Too many people attribute what the devil is doing to God. By the way, this is blasphemy. When sickness comes, some religious person who is ignorant of the Word of God will make the statement, "Oh God is trying to tell you something." Or when someone dies, or loses a valuable possession through theft or robbery, or some other bad event in life occurs—people who do not know any better will make accusations that God is the one who brought this tragedy, pain, or loss. There is a problem with that type theology. The Word of God soundly refutes the idea of God needing to stoop down to a fleshy level to deal with people. Although, in many instances in Scripture God may have stepped back or removed a hedge of protection — admittedly it was the devil that actually performed the evil deed.

In the Book of James, Chapter 1 and verse 17 you find: **"Every good gift and every perfect gift is from above, and** *cometh down from the Father of lights, with whom is no variableness, neither shadow of turning."* Two points must be discussed regarding this passage of scripture: first, God's standard of giving only good and perfect gifts, and second, God's stability in giving gifts that are fixed and settled.

God is a quality God. He only gives the best and does the best for His children. He has a track record of not just supplying needs, but also of even granting desires of the heart. Think back to the children of Israel when they were in the wilderness. Even though, God protected them, guided them, and FED THEM with manna each day; He did not stop there. When they began to grumble and complain and lust after flesh, what did He do? He provided them with more than enough quail! (Numbers 11)

El Sheddai – God Is All Sufficient
He Is More Than Enough

Think about it! You don't just serve the God of Enough, but you serve the Ephesians 3:20 God! He is the God of "More Than Enough". *"Now unto him that is able to do exceeding abundantly above all that we ask or think, according to the*

power that worketh in us," (Ephesians 3:20). Yes, God is able to do exceeding and abundantly above (more than) all you could ask, think, desire, imagine, or conceive. Because He is God, he knows the fine workings of your spirit and soul. He understands your heart and your emotions. And because He is the Father and He has the Father's heart he will lovingly and freely give good gifts unto you.

Also, you must recognize that God's gifts are fixed and settled. Remember, He said, ***"I am the Lord and I changeth not."*** (Malachi 3:6) God does not change his mind in regards to the gift of power that he has invested in you. ***"For the gifts and callings of God are without repentance."*** (Romans 11:29) You may waver. You may even change. But the gifts and callings of God are constant. God has created a standard (called His Will). Whenever you operate and exist in His Will, you can operate in the gifts and callings He has decided for your life. But, whenever you get out of the will of God—the gifts and callings do not follow you, they remain constant. Yes, there are still reserved for you back "in His will." And just soon as you submit to the Word of God and the Will of God, you will see the manifestation of the same gifts God has already promised.

Many Spirit-filled believers have been crying out for "more" power. There are people who claim to be seeking the Holy Ghost trying to get "more" power. When one has received the Holy Ghost as recorded in the Book of Acts (***but ye shall receive power***, Act 1:8), they already have the power of God.

What often takes place is that well-intentioned believers begin looking for something that is not lost. They begin to attempt to bring something from the outside within them—but the bottom line is that the "power" that some believers search for is not outside, but within. When the Holy Spirit has made His abode in a person's heart, He does not have to be summoned from the heavenlies. Paul told Timothy what to do with the gift of God within him, In II Timothy 1: 6 the Word of God reads: ***"Wherefore I put thee in remembrance that thou stir up the gift of God, which is in thee by the putting on of my hands."*** Timothy is told to "stir up the gift of God" that is within him. This may also be translated to "keep in full flame" the grace gift which came from God.

When I think of "stirring up a gift" and "keeping in full flame," I am reminded of a cook preparing food that has been in the refrigerator. Foods that have been stored in a refrigerator have a tendency of gelling and becoming solid. Yet, when heat is applied to these foods they become manageable again. They are now able to be stirred and prepared. Oftentimes, life can be the same way. Situations, circumstances, and conditions, can cause the heart and soul to grow cold, indifferent, and unresponsive. Many complain when it seems that they are under severe attack from the enemy. Do not be deceived by the devil's devices. What the devil said would take you out, really is what is going to bring you in. That's right, the test that you're going through is becoming your testimony. Learn how to turn the mess in your life into your message. You are in control when it comes to how you will react or respond to pressure or heat in your life. You can allow these to be stepping stones or stumbling blocks. It's all up to you!

Learn To Embrace The Fire!

  Welcome the heat! Realizing who you are and whose you are—you can't be defeated! Just like God delivered the Hebrew boys out of the fiery furnace, God will also deliver you. Remember, not only did they go through the fire, but as they came out the Word of God says that their hair was not singed neither did their clothes have the scent of smoke. Don't tell me God isn't an awesome God!

  I have endured many challenges in my walk with God. However, in the midst of every trial and adversity that I have faced – God's power has kept me. Yes, the indwelling presence of the Spirit of God has kept a smile on my face when circumstances encouraged me to frown or cry. The Spirit of God will strengthen you to not bend or break when you go through trials and tribulations. You must be willing to allow the Spirit to be the Comforter that God promised He would send.

I have learned to embrace the fire. For as I consider that God will not permit anything to occur that He has not fashioned me to endure, I am comforted to know that after the fire I will be better. In the words made popular by Pastor Marvin Sapp, "I'm stronger. I'm wiser. I'm better."

"Beloved, think it not strange concerning the fiery trial which is to try you, as though some strange thing happened unto you: But rejoice, inasmuch as ye are partakers of Christ's sufferings; that, when His glory shall be revealed, ye may be glad with exceeding joy." (I Peter 4:12-13)

If Christ had to face the heat, so do you. And remember, as Christ was victorious even now in life so shall you be. And remember, your victory is because the "greater one" lives in you! Understand that you are engaged in a war. Your entire life from the cradle to the grave is spiritual warfare. Within the war are events called battles. When you begin to focus and concentrate on the battles and not the war you open yourself up for defeat.

The scripture in Romans 8:37, declares that you are more than a conqueror! When you hold onto this attitude and refuse to relinquish anymore territory to the enemy, you will begin to taste the victory that has already been prepared for you. The bottom line is that you must learn how to step back and look at the "big picture". Stop getting lost in the fine details that come to distract you and hinder you. My secretary gave me a word one day. She related to me that God told her "Output was the focus". That blessed me. What she was saying was to stop allowing the daily frustrations to hinder you from concentrating on the final victory that belongs to you. What you do is what matters, not what is being done to you!

As you consider Shadrach, Meshech, and Abednego, most often people always concentrate on them being in the fiery furnace. But, look at the output. What happened? They came out of the fire with no hurt or harm. They didn't even have the scent of smoke on their garments. Don't tell me God isn't an awesome God!

Remember, you are conquerors THROUGH HIM! Excuse me, you are more than conquerors! Jesus Christ is responsible for your victory! As long as you trust in Him, continue to abide in Him, you will have no need to worry or fret about situations, circumstances or conditions. No matter what you think, what you hear, what you see, or what you feel – Do not be moved! The conclusion of the matter is already settled! The devil is the loser! You are the winner!

Spirit-Filled, Not Spirit-Led

The presence of the Holy Spirit in your life does not make you a puppet or a robot. The Spirit of God is ready, willing and available, but not controlling. You must yield yourself to the leadership of the Spirit. The Holy Spirit will not force you to live right or do right. God has given you a free will. It is up to you to respect the teaching and leading of the Spirit of God. Some of the functions of the Holy Spirit in the life of a believer are to lead, guide, direct, teach and intercede.

Often when a believer sins or steps outside of the will of God, by-standers will say that they aren't really saved or that they don't have the Holy Ghost. They declare that the Holy Ghost would not let them act or speak in an ungodly way. Yet, the Apostle Paul described the struggles in a Christian's life.

"For that which I do I allow not: for what I would, that do I not; but what I hate, that do I. 16 If then I do that which I would not, I consent unto the law that it is good. Now then it is no more I that do it, but sin that dwelleth in me. For I know that in me (that is, in my flesh,) dwelleth no good thing: for to will is present with me; but how to perform that which is good I find not. For the good that I would I do not: but the evil which I would not, that I do. Now if I do that I

would not, it is no more I that do it, but sin that dwelleth in me." (Romans 7:15-20)

We can agree that Paul was a Spirit-filled believer, yet evidently there were points in his life were he did not obey the Spirit within. Too often this happens in the lives of everyday believers. It is the intent and desire of the devil to make those acts of disobedience happen so often, that you end up giving up trying to live right.

God Has Not Given Up On You!

Have you ever felt that you had gone too far and that God had given up on you? Have you ever felt that you had disobeyed God to the extent that there was no more help or hope for you? Have you ever felt empty, lonely and absent of God's Spirit within? Some would encourage you to even believe that you had a reprobate mind. Well, there is a simple way to check if you have that type of mind.

Every time you sin or fall short of God's will – how do you feel? How do you respond? Do you feel guilty? Are you ashamed? Does hurt prevail in your heart and mind? If you can answer yes, then your mind is not reprobated. God has not given up on you. He made be disappointed by your choices but He still is allowing His Spirit to reveal His true plan for your life.

A reprobate mind is one that has lost consciousness of sin. This type person can exist in sin and feel fine with it. This is a dangerous place to live. Always look for that small voice on the inside still whispering God's perfect will and patiently calling out to you to return to the place where God intends you to be. Don't be tricked by the enemy to continue down a path that leads you further away from God's desire for you.

You have to remind yourself that this life is a continual warfare! Every day you are fighting the *"good fight of faith"* This is what Paul told Timothy: **"Fight the good fight of faith, lay hold on eternal life, whereunto thou art also called, and hast professed a good profession before many witnesses."** (I Timothy 6:12) Yes, each day of your life, your faith is actually on trial. The devil wants so badly to prove to God that you will give up, you will give in. Your job is to be wise enough to recognize the enemy in his deception and keep fighting. Keep struggling. Keep pushing.

There is a way to be Spirit-Led and Spirit-filled. You must do what the Apostle Paul told Timothy to do. **"Wherefore I put thee in remembrance that thou stir up the gift of God,**

which is in thee by the putting on of my hands." (II Timothy 1:6) Yes, you must stir up the gift that is within you. You must operate in ways that prompt you to be sensitive to and obedient to the Spirit of God. The Spirit of God that is within you is urging you and pleading with you to Hear His voice and walk into the purpose and destiny that God has designed for your life.

You Don't Have To Walk After The Flesh!

There is analogy that I have used for years that is so simple, yet I believe its truth to be profound. The Mississippi River is a great River that runs the expanse of the United States beginning up north in Minnesota and continuing down south through Louisiana and Mississippi to the Gulf of Mexico. There are points where the river runs deep and wide. However, I have told people there is a way to guarantee that you never drown in the Mississippi River. As long as you abide in the State of Georgia it is impossible for you to drown in the Mississippi River. I can make this guarantee simply because Georgia is many miles east of the Mississippi River. So, no matter whether you are in Atlanta, Savannah, Macon or even Columbus – you are safe.

This comparison is used in walking in the Spirit versus walking after the flesh. Paul encourages the Galatians as he writes, **"This I say then, Walk in the Spirit, and ye shall not fulfil the lust of the flesh. For the flesh lusteth against the Spirit, and the Spirit against the flesh: and these are contrary the one to the other: so that ye cannot do the things that ye would."** (Galatians 5:16-17) As long as you obey the leading of the Holy Spirit, it is impossible for you to abide in sin. The problem is that there are instances where even the best saints fall short at walking in complete obedience.

You may have mastered abstaining from some of the obvious works of the flesh such as cursing, being drunken, or committing sexual sins such as lust, fornication or adultery. But, what about relationship matters? How do you treat others? Do you participate in gossip and tale-bearing? Do you love those who dislike you and say and do mean things to you? Do you pray for those who misuse and abuse you?

What about the gray areas? Is the Spirit pleased and is God glorified when you laugh at jokes that demean, or portray others in negative and even vulgar manners? What about the songs you listen to on the radio and the television shows you watch on T.V? How about simple things like coming to work late or leaving early, but never adjusting the time on your time card. Isn't that really stealing? Or even the fruit that you eat while passing through the produce section, but you don't pay for at the check-out?

Even deeper than that, how sensitive are you to the Spirit of God in your life? Did you realize that it is a sin not to obey the prompting of the Spirit of God? Do you pray as often as you should? Do you participate in evangelism and missions at the level that God desires for you to? How often do you read, meditate and study the Holy Scriptures? How important is the ministry of giving to you as demonstrated through your tithing, freewill offerings and seed sowing opportunities?

Yes, it is so easy to get distracted and not walk in the Spirit 24-7. God is always speaking, but are you always listening? When the Spirit of God is attempting to do His job in your life and you choose to disobey this grieves Him. **"And grieve not the Holy Spirit of God, whereby ye are sealed unto the day of redemption."** (Ephesians 4:30) When those times come that you realize you have strayed away from God's perfect will and not yielded to the leading of the Spirit of God – repent. Right then and there, apologize to God and immediately change your actions. That immediate change will keep you from drowning and bless you to not only be Spirit-filled but Spirit-led.

Dunamis In Your Life

Dunamis is the very ability of God. This is God's power. And in Acts 1:8, this is the same power that God promised to believers. *"But ye shall receive power, after that the Holy Ghost is come upon you: and ye shall be witnesses unto me both in Jerusalem, and in all Judaea, and in Samaria, and unto the uttermost part of the earth."* God desires that believers be equipped in the earth realm to be victorious and effective in their daily walk. This ability comes through the presence of the Holy Spirit in your life.

Seven Blessings Of The Holy Spirit

There are 7 blessings of the Holy Spirit in your life.
1. Effective Witness
2. Effect Change
3. Overcoming / Victorious Living
4. Gifts and Fruit
5. Worship
6. Reception
7. Intercession

The fullness of the Holy Spirit in a believer's life empowers them to be a more effective witness in the earth realm. Just imagine, with a bicycle you can ride across town in a half hour time span. But, that same distance can be traveled in a car in possibly 10 or 15 minutes. Use that analogy to see the difference the Holy Spirit can make in the life of a believer. You are equipped with a supernatural force that can help you to accomplish more for the kingdom of God. You can go further, you can last longer, and you can accomplish more all for God's glory.

The Spirit Brings Change

The Spirit of God makes you a more effective witness. That was the promise made in Acts 1:8. When you are endued with power from on high, look for change at home, in your neighborhood, on your job, at the church, in the city, and all across the nation where you travel. You will be able to reach people regardless of racial, ethnic, social, or sexual orientation or background. God will make you a powerhouse witness tool in the earth realm.

Your life will change. You will experience overcoming power like never before. Even when challenges come in your life, the power of the Holy Ghost will cause you to rise up and still walk in victory. Weapons may form, but they won't prosper. Floods may come, but you won't drown. The manifested presence of God's Spirit in your life will give you a new way to handle life! His dynamite power *"dunamis"* will make you an explosive force to be reckoned with.

The fruit of the Spirit and the gifts of the Spirit will be magnified in your life. You will begin to operate in ways that may astound others. You should not be surprised, just know that it is God working in and through you for His glory. The fruit of the Spirit as revealed in Galatians 5:22-23 will guide your life, **"But the fruit of the Spirit is love, joy, peace, longsuffering, gentleness, goodness, faith, Meekness, temperance: against such there is no law."** You will express these virtues painlessly and effortlessly in your everyday living.

As you grow in the things of God, He will begin to manifest His gifts in your life. There are three areas of spiritual gifts that God desires to operate through you: gifts that say something, gifts that do something, and gifts that reveal something. He wants you to be knowledgeable about His gifts and ministries. *"Now concerning spiritual gifts, brethren, I would not have you ignorant."* (I Corinthians 12:1)

Always remember, the gifts are God's and not yours. You cannot pick and choose which gifts suit you and which are your favorite to utilize. That is God's prerogative. He chooses when, who, how, and to what extent His gifts operate in believers. Your job is simply always to be ready, willing, and able to be a vessel for the Master's use.

"Now there are diversities of gifts, but the same Spirit. And there are differences of administrations, but the same Lord. And there are diversities of operations, but it is the same God which worketh all in all. But the manifestation of the Spirit is given to every man to profit withal. For to one is given by the Spirit the word of wisdom ; to another the word of knowledge by the same Spirit; To another faith by the same Spirit ; to another the gifts of healing by the same Spirit; To another the working of miracles ; to another prophecy ; to another discerning of spirits ; to another divers kinds of tongues; to another the interpretation of tongues: But all these worketh that one and the selfsame

Spirit, dividing to every man severally as he will." (I Corinthians 12:4-11)

Worship is intimacy with God. Your spirit communing and fellowshipping with God's Spirit is awesome. Worship is not just an act or event that takes place when you attend church. But, God wants the words of the Sunday School song to be realized in your relationship with Him: *"And He walks with me, and He talks with me, and He tells me I am His own..."* When you are filled with God's Spirit, worship is not a chore or an isolated event but it is simply a way of life because of the deposit of His Spirit that has been made within you.

Some have confused the Holy Ghost with mere emotions. But, the Spirit of God is much more. He does not just make you shout and "get happy" in church. God gave us emotions and emotions are good. It is wonderful to express joy in the sanctuary. Am I a "holy roller"? - Very much so, and not ashamed. I love to run, leap, jump and dance, but the Spirit of God is much more than just these physical expressions of my emotions. He is the Comforter! He is the revealer. He is the teacher. He is the intercessor.

"Howbeit when he, the Spirit of truth, is come, He will guide you into all truth: for He shall not speak of himself; but

whatsoever He shall hear, that shall He speak: and He will shew you things to come." (John 16:13)

"But as it is written, Eye hath not seen, nor ear heard, neither have entered into the heart of man, the things which God hath prepared for them that love him. 10 But God hath revealed them unto us by his Spirit: for the Spirit searcheth all things, yea, the deep things of God. 11 For what man knoweth the things of a man, save the spirit of man which is in him? even so the things of God knoweth no man, but the Spirit of God. 12 Now we have received, not the spirit of the world, but the spirit which is of God; that we might know the things that are freely given to us of God." (I Corinthians 2:9-12)

The Perfect Prayer Partner

One of the most awesome functions of the Spirit of God is as intercessor. Prayer is our direct line of communication with God. When we pray, we expect God to not only hear us but to answer us favorably. However, sometimes we don't pray as we should. That is the wonderful comfort of having a prayer partner with perfect vision, knowledge and perception.

"Likewise the Spirit also helpeth our infirmities: for we know not what we should pray for as we ought : but the Spirit itself maketh intercession for us with groanings which cannot be uttered." (Romans 8:26)

Since the Holy Spirit is the Spirit of God, He knows the mind of God. When I allow the Holy Spirit to guide my prayer, it is just like God praying to Himself on my behalf. He will only speak His will. So, my prayer will not be based upon my fleshly desires or whims, but it will be His will.

When I pray, I want the assurance of God hearing and answering my prayer. I have learned that the way that my prayer can be guaranteed is to allow the Spirit of God to intercede for me. That is why I agree with the Apostle Paul when he said in I Corinthians 14:15: *"What is it then? I will pray with the spirit, and I will pray with the understanding also: I will sing with the spirit, and I will sing with the understanding also."*

When I engage in prayer, I have learned how to pray in my own understanding. And then, I sit and I patiently await the presence of God to move upon me so that I may yield myself to allow His Spirit to pray as well. Praying is not always just telling God, but it is also listening to God. If prayer is communication with God, then God should be permitted to speak as well.

Interceding is just one of the many functions of the Holy Spirit in the life of believers. Learn all you can about His purpose and functions in the earth realm. Realize a new way of living as you live in the Spirit.

The *"dunamis"* in your life should simply be embraced. You don't have to struggle to be yourself. Usually when people are uncertain and struggling to prove themselves it is because they are trying to be something or someone they are not. Recognize that your heavenly Father has made an awesome investment in you. Remind yourself that His investment has been tailored to fit your personality and expression. One spirit – many manifestations!

THE WORK OF THE HOLY GHOST...

* Confirms salvation	Eph. 4:30
* Speaks through people	Acts 1:16
* Is a witness	Acts 5:32
* Purifies the heart	Acts 15:9
* Is a keeper	II Timothy 1:14
* Is a convincer	John 16:8
* Is a revealer, guide	John 16:13
* Is a teacher	Luke 24:49, John 14:26
* Is a Comforter	John 16:7, John 14:16
* Is an intercessor	Romans 8:26
* Endues one with power	Acts 1:8
* Gives utterance	Acts 2:4
* Purifies the heart by faith	Acts 15:9
* Indwells believers	Romans 8:11
* Gives gifts	I Corinthians 12:3-11
* Gives joy	Romans 14:17
* Anoints	I John 2:20, 27
* Baptizes	Acts 2:17-41, I Cor. 12:13
* Comforts the church	Acts 9:31
* Sanctifies the church	Romans 15:16

The Baptism Of Power

There are so many expressions that people have used regarding the move of the Holy Spirit in a believer's life. Did you "catch" the Holy Ghost? Did you "get happy"? Did you "catch on fire"? Did you "shout"?

But, the real truth of the matter, the Baptism in the Holy Ghost is an experience that should be ongoing in believer's lives. To baptize means to submerge or immerse. So, just allowing the Spirit to influence one area of your life does not dictate being baptized in the Spirit. When you are submerged or immersed, all of you should get wet. This is God's intent and plan for your life. He wants all of your life to be affected by the work of the Holy Ghost. The presence and work of the Holy Ghost in your life should not be limited to an event but it should be present every day.

The Holy Spirit Ushers In Change

When you experience the fullness of the Spirit of God in your life, He gives direction to you. No longer do you need a rule book (or people) to regulate and guide your life. He (the

Spirit of God) will direct you in what to say and what not to say. He will tell you where you should and should not go. He will reveal to you the people that you should connect with and He will also show you the people with whom you need to experience the ministry of "disconnect". He will help you to pray. He will tell you how to dress and carry yourself in a way that pleases God.

All of this involves "change" that many people are not ready for. Change is not always comfortable and it takes the control away from you. You are no longer in charge and running things. The Spirit is. You have to command your flesh (which wants to rule and dominate) to surrender to your spirit which is born again and under the influence and control of the Holy Spirit.

Listen to the voice of the Spirit

I remember visiting a friend's church and they were in the midst of a great revival. After the Word of God had been preached there were people at the altar with various ministry needs. I had been beckoned to the altar to assist. As I went forward, they asked me to minister to this man that was "seeking the Holy Ghost". I said okay and began to pray with the gentleman. As I began to pray, the Spirit of God spoke very clearly to me, "He is not saved!" I ignored the voice (foolish huh?) and kept praying. After a few more minutes the Spirit of God spoke again into my ear, "He is not saved!"

The church service was quite loud. The organ was playing, the drums were beating, there were people shouting and dancing, others were receiving prayer. The man was bobbing back and forth, perspiring heavily, and calling on Jesus. At this point, I stopped and shook the man to get his attention. I asked him, "Sir, what is your name?" After he responded, I simply asked him was he saved. He responded, "No"! Of course, you know I was floored. I could feel the Spirit of God smiling at me with the expressive words: *I told you so!*

I then asked him if he wanted to be saved. He said that he did. I then began to minister salvation to him based upon the scripture found in Romans 10:9-13:

"That if thou shalt confess with thy mouth the Lord Jesus, and shalt believe in thine heart that God hath raised him from the dead, thou shalt be saved . For with the heart man believeth unto righteousness; and with the mouth confession is made unto salvation. For the scripture saith, Whosoever believeth on him shall not be ashamed. For there is no difference between the Jew and the Greek: for the same

Lord over all is rich unto all that call upon him. For whosoever shall call upon the name of the Lord shall be saved."

After he prayed with me and accepted the Lord Jesus Christ as His personal Savior, I laid my hands upon him and almost immediately he began to speak in other tongues as the Spirit gave Him utterance. I learned such a valuable lesson in this experience. Learn to listen to the voice of the Spirit! The baptism in the Holy Ghost is a free gift for all believers. Not only was this a life-changing experience for the man, but I was richly blessed by God in learning strict obedience to His voice.

Experiencing the Baptism in the Holy Ghost is a wonderful experience but when flesh (people) gets involved it can be challenging and unrewarding. Let me share some guidelines with you as you either experience the Baptism in the Holy Ghost for the first time yourself or use these points as ministry tools in your personal ministry as you minister to others who are seeking the fullness of God's Spirit.

You Can Receive The Baptism Now!

The only prerequisite to experiencing the baptism in the Holy Ghost is salvation. The gift is for all believers. Some people have thought that this experience was for certain denominations. That is absolutely not true. God desires all of His children to experience the fullness of His Spirit in their life on a daily basis. See the response in God's Word to a message Peter preached, *"Now when they heard this, they were pricked in their heart, and said unto Peter and to the rest of the apostles, Men and brethren, what shall we do? Then Peter said unto them, Repent, and be baptized every one of you in the name of Jesus Christ for the remission of sins, and ye shall receive the gift of the Holy Ghost."* (Acts 2:37-38) If you are a believer, then you are a prime candidate for the Baptism in the Holy Ghost.

Understand that the Spirit is already given. You are not waiting on some great release from God. The Spirit of God is actively present in the earth realm today. When you accepted the Lord in your heart and received salvation you were ready then and there. There was another instance in God's Word where believers had received salvation but not the Spirit baptism.

"Now when the apostles which were at Jerusalem heard that Samaria had received the word of God, they sent unto them Peter and John: Who, when they were come down,

prayed for them, that they might receive the Holy Ghost: (For as yet he was fallen upon none of them: only they were baptized in the name of the Lord Jesus.) Then laid they their hands on them, and they received the Holy Ghost". (Acts 8:14-17) You don't have to wait any longer! The Holy Spirit has been given and all you have to do is desire to receive.

Some people have debated over whether they can receive the baptism in the Holy Ghost on their own or do they have to have someone else present. God is much too big to be limited by finite man. If you desire the fullness of God, then pray and receive. However in the early church, a framework of "laying on of hands" was demonstrated and utilized by the apostles.

"Then laid they their hands on them, and they received the Holy Ghost." (Acts 8:17)

"And when Paul had laid his hands upon them, the Holy Ghost came on them; and they spake with tongues, and prophesied." (Acts 19:6)

Then comes the big challenge: making your flesh "sit down" and allowing your spirit to simply yield to what God is doing! Some have allowed the Baptism in the Holy Spirit to be a great ordeal and challenge when it really is only an act of submission. Don't make it one thing when it really is something else. Some have the idea that they are looking for tongues, however, that was NOT the promise that was given. The promise was power! If you change your search, you will find more than you ever dreamed.

God Promised Power! Not Tongues!

When you go to the shoe store to select tennis shoes, do you look for the tongues or the actual shoe. Of course, you are looking for the make-up of the actual shoe. The tongue of the shoe is only a part of the shoe that you are searching for. The same is with the Spirit of God. Don't be misled by simply looking for a tongue. Pray to God for the promised power and the tongue is just an additional blessing that comes along with the power.

You can even consider the tongue as a receipt. When you make a purchase at a store, you are not walking in looking for the receipt. You are looking for the product that you are trying to buy. The receipt is simply what they give you when you walk out of the door as proof that you purchased the item.

Another challenge that many people face is the fear of receiving something false. If you read throughout the Word of God, you will find a plethora of scripture verses exhorting you to **"Fear not"**! Remember, who you are and whose you are. You have no reason of fearing something false or fake if your heart is sincere and pure towards God.

"If a son shall ask bread of any of you that is a father, will he give him a stone? or if he ask a fish, will he for a fish give him a serpent? Or if he shall ask an egg, will he offer him a scorpion? If ye then, being evil, know how to give good gifts unto your children: how much more shall your heavenly Father give the Holy Spirit to them that ask him?" (Luke 11:11-13)

If you are God's child and you are sincerely seeking His promise for your life, He will not deny you. He loves you enough to give you not just the answer to your prayer, but blessings upon blessings besides that.

The Spirit of God will prompt you. Yes, words will form upon your lips that you have never recited or learned before. This is the miracle of God. It is not made up! And, no man can "teach" you what to say. You simply yield your tongue just like all of the believers in the early church and as countless believers over the ages have done and are still doing. It's real! Let the Spirit tell you what to say!

"And they were all filled with the Holy Ghost, and began to speak with other tongues, as the Spirit gave them utterance." (Acts 2:4)

"While Peter yet spake these words, the Holy Ghost fell on all them which heard the word. And they of the circumcision which believed were astonished, as many as came with Peter, because that on the Gentiles also was poured out the gift of the Holy Ghost. For they heard them speak with tongues, and magnify God. Then answered Peter, Can any man forbid water, that these should not be baptized, which have received the Holy Ghost as well as we?" (Acts 10:44-47)

"And when Paul had laid his hands upon them, the Holy Ghost came on them; and they spake with tongues, and prophesied." (Acts 19:6)

Open Your Mouth In Expectation!

One of the things that has amazed me over the years during ministry is people's posture. I have often asked myself and asked others, how is it that you plan to speak with your mouth closed! I have seen many people come to the altar to receive the baptism in the Holy Ghost and just stand there. They stand there and wait. I don't know if they think God is going to pry their mouth open or what!

I really appreciate the scriptures found in the Book of Job that talk about the latter rain which is symbolic of the Holy Spirit. This is a method that I encourage believers to employ when seeking to be filled with the Holy Ghost.

"Unto me men gave ear, and waited, and kept silence at my counsel. After my words they spake not again; and my speech dropped upon them. And they waited for me as for the rain; and they opened their mouth wide as for the latter rain." (Job 29:21-23)

The simple steps that I found in this passage of scripture that have blessed countless believers are:
1. Hear God
2. Trust God
3. Surrender To God
4. Wait On God
5. Expect God
6. Let God

And all of this is done, with your mouth open! Some may wonder why it is important that your mouth be open.

Well, it is my belief that if I am about to use my mouth it should be in the most convenient position to be operable.

When I speak, I do so with my mouth open. When I am preparing to allow God to speak through me, I do so with my mouth open. That is true expectation and active faith.

Finally, one of the best pieces of advice for a believer seeking to experience the baptism in the Holy Ghost is to avoid confusing people. A great hindrance to the move of God is people. Everyone comes with their own prescription or recommendation, and most of what people have to say is not based on any scripture.

"While Peter yet spake these words, the Holy Ghost fell on all them which heard the word." (Acts 10:44)
"But if we hope for that we see not, then do we with patience wait for it." (Romans 8:25)

"But ye, beloved, building up yourselves on your most holy faith, praying in the Holy Ghost," (Jude 20)

I enjoy telling the story about the young lady who was standing at the altar "trying to get saved"! The altar worker asked her what was wrong and what was hindering her from simply receiving the Lord in her heart. The young lady replied that she was waiting to feel the gush of wind come through like on the day of Pentecost because that was how it happened for her grandmother. The altar worker attempted to let her know that her salvation was not based upon "feeling" or "emotion" but simply her faith in God's grace.

The young lady then described her grandmother's conversion experience. And she said that she wanted to experience God like her grandmother. Her grandmother's testimony was that she was at the altar "calling on Jesus" and that she felt the Spirit like a mighty wind come in and then she was saved. That sounds like a wonderful experience. However, the truth of the matter is the part of her grandmother's testimony that is untold. *It was January and the temperature was quite cold. She had been in the service at the altar of a small wooden church for quite some time clapping and calling on Jesus. She was sweating and nervous and excited all at the same time. All of a sudden, someone opened the back door of the church and a wind blew in and that was what she "felt".*

You cannot allow other people's experiences dictate how God will move in your life. God is a one-on-one God. He is as individual and specific to you as you are different from those around you. People can contaminate ministry and confuse young believers if care is not taken. Although, well-intentioned it is wise to not allow too many people to give directives when it involves receiving the baptism in the Holy Ghost.

"Beware lest any man spoil you through philosophy and vain deceit, after the tradition of men, after the rudiments of the world, and not after Christ." (Colossians 2:8)

Just imagine a crowd of people with a young believer standing in the middle. What would you expect the believer to do or to receive after hearing the following commands? "Let go"! "Hold on"! "Call Jesus"! "Be Still"! "Stretch Out"! "Clap Your Hands"! "Leap For Joy"! "There It Is"! "It's On The Way"! "You Got It"!

Yes, that is truly a confusing scene. But, it is a scene that happens too often. People who are receiving the baptism in the Holy Spirit don't need cheerleaders or directors. They simply need to know God's Word, believe God's Word, and receive God's Word.

SPIRIT FILLED CONFESSION

I believe with all my heart, and I confess with my mouth, that the Word of God is true, the Word of God is eternal, the Word of God is alive, the Word of God is changeless. I choose to set my life in agreement with the Word of God.

I confess that I am saved by faith in God's wonderful grace. Jesus is the Lord and Savior of my life. I believe that He was resurrected after three days and three nights by the power of God as the Scriptures declare. His Word has saved me.

I now receive the Holy Spirit by faith. I accept this free gift from God with joy and excitement. I confess that it was the Spirit of God that drew me to salvation.

I proclaim that since the Day of Pentecost the Holy Spirit has already been given in this dispensation and I am available to receive Him in me now. As the Holy Spirit fills me I will speak with tongues and magnify God. I will manifest the power that God has endued me with in my home, community, church and abroad.

I yield my tongue to speak as the Spirit gives me utterance. I command my tongue to speak not unto men, but unto God. In the spirit, I speak mysteries. I decide right now to be a fulfillment of the Word of God, as His Spirit is poured out upon all flesh. I choose now to allow rivers of living water to flow out of my innermost being.

I proclaim that I am right now a Spirit-filled believer. The Holy Spirit of God dwells in me by faith and power! He teaches me, He guides me, He comforts me, He sanctifies me, He keeps me. He is my intercessor and my gift of God!

Personal Note From Pastor Porter...

God loves you enough to save you and fill you with His Spirit even as you read this book. You don't need an audience. All you need is faith in God to receive His wonderful promise which is to all who believe. It is great when you can go to a church service and people are there to pray with you and minister with you. However, if you have faith to believe the above confession – then God will fill you with His Spirit even now. God gave me these words some years ago, and down through the years I have even experienced people actually receiving the Baptism in the Holy Spirit while confessing these words during worship services. **Trust God and Be ye filled with the Holy Ghost!**

O'NEAL STALLWORTH PORTER

Since 1989, **O'Neal Stallworth Porter** has served as the senior pastor of the Fellowship Church in Eight Mile, Alabama. Fellowship Church is a growing non-denominational ministry located near Mobile, Alabama. Pastor Porter, a native Mobilian, is a graduate of the University of Alabama (Tuscaloosa) with a Bachelors of Arts degree in Communications and a graduate of the Alabama State University with a Masters of Education degree in Educational Administration. He is an active member of the Port City United Voices (Mobile, Alabama Chapter of the Gospel Music Workshop of America). He is also founder and director of the gospel singing group: FAITH – *Friends Are In The House*. Pastor Porter is an anointed teacher, psalmist, composer, choral director, gospel music workshop clinician and speaker. One of the special areas that God has gifted him is to lead "Praise Into Worship" Seminars where he teaches praise teams, choirs and entire congregations biblical foundations and practical applications of entering into the presence of God. He is the author of an awesome book entitled, *"Praise Is What I Do – No Other Option"*. His second volume: *"God's Power In The Believer"* is scheduled to be released during January 2011. He has served as host for the TBN (Trinity Broadcasting Network - Christian Television) Program. He and his wife Sabrina are the proud parents of four wonderful children: Kymberly Dawnique, Brooke O'Neal, Morgan Char'les, and Charles Van James.

CONTACT INFO

Pastor Porter is a multi-gifted vessel in the Body of Christ. He brings a wealth of wisdom, knowledge and experience in the Word (teaching and preaching) Ministry as well as the Music (composing, directing, singing) Ministry. To secure him to come and be a blessing at a service or event, please utilize the following contact information...

Pastor O'Neal Porter

P.O. Box 13125

Eight Mile, Alabama 36633

(251) 281-7643

www.onealporter.com - onealporter@yahoo.com

WEBSITE   **EMAIL**